D1431233

i

"For I know the plans I have for you," declares the LORD, "plans to prosper you and not to harm you, plans to give you hope and a future. Then you will call on me and come and pray to me, and I will listen to you."

~Jeremiah 29:11-12

A
BETTER
PLAN

Stories That Inspire

2018

Trust in the LORD with all your heart;
do not depend on your own understanding.
Seek his will in all you do,
and he will show you which path to take.

~Proverbs 3:5-6

Introduction

*M*any times in my life I have been humbled by opportunities to witness God's blessing and miracles; whether in my own life or through the life of a family member, friend or someone else. I cannot and will not profess to know how or why God does what He does, He is after all, God. However, I do know that He is present, and we can experience a glimpse of His love and compassion if we only get to know Him through His son Jesus.

I decided to publish this book because I knew there were others like me who had a story to tell about God's amazing work. Others who had witnessed first-hand his blessings. Normal people like me and like you that had a story of faith to share.

The contributing authors in this book were brave enough to share their own stories and insights. They did this with the hope that other people, like you, would find something to take away. Something that would inspire you to make the important changes in your life. To understand that what you are going through does not define you but can certainly refine you to start living with and for a better plan. You can do it; however, you must be willing to believe, take action, and start pursuing your greatest purpose. I would like to tell you that it is going to be easy, but it is not. I would like to say that there is nothing special about the contributors to this book, but that would also not be true. Yet, it would also be false for you to believe that there is nothing special about you, too.

You were created with precision, purpose, and your own unique talents. You were also given the ability to know, act on, and use those talents to become greater and stronger in your own way. Just accept, remember, and most importantly believe this, "I can do all things through Christ, who strengthens me." Philippians 4:13 (*NKJV*). As I always say, "Through faith and action, ALL things are possible."

Now, let's get YOU started on following a better plan.

Mike Rodriguez

"It's not that you can't find your purpose,
You are simply looking in the wrong direction."
-    Mike Rodriguez

Chapter 1

Your Life Is a Gift to You
By Mike Rodriguez

Where you are in your life right now is only temporary.
It's up to you to let it become permanent.

This applies to all situations and to all people. Whether you are on top of the world right now, facing a tragic loss or even if you feel that you are just existing, it is only temporary. If you are at a point in your life that is not "where" you expected or "what" you expected, that is certainly understandable. It is, however, up to you to let where you are, become permanent. Life doesn't always present good situations, nor are they easy. Regardless of how you view where you are, you must believe that what is happening, is happening for a reason. When facing a tough time or going through a bad situation, let yourself feel whatever emotions you are going through, but don't let them overtake you. Tough times will not last, when God is in control.

Most of the challenges that I have lived through, when I trace them back, were usually a result of the

1

consequences of my decisions (or indecisions) which preceded my actions. Yet, I have also learned that God places us in situations or allows situations to happen, for us to get through, so He can get through to us. Situations that you are in may not make sense to you today, but they will later.

All of life's experiences serve a higher purpose - to bring us closer to God. He is indeed mysterious and when we seek to understand Him from a human perspective, nothing that has happened or that will happen in our lives could ever make sense, because God is not human. He is the almighty creator of the universe!

In fact, He tells us:

> "For My thoughts are not your thoughts,
> Nor are your ways My ways," declares the LORD.
> "For as the heavens are higher than the earth,
> So are My ways higher than your ways
> And My thoughts than your thoughts.
> – Isaiah 55:8-9

I find that most of us rationalize with and analyze our creator, based on what we feel, want, need or hope to happen. This is where we get side-tracked on our journey through life, especially when we are going through tough times. We must learn to understand that in life, we are either moving closer towards God or we are moving further from Him. Let me clarify that He is always with us and never leaves us. Regardless of where we are in life, what we are doing or what we are going through, he is always there.

When we do things to move further away from God, this means that we are choosing to think, speak or act in a way that is not compatible with allowing Him to go to work in our lives. This usually involves us doing something that we shouldn't be doing, having a lack of faith in general or just living our lives in our own way, according to the world and our will. Awareness of our selfishness, creates an awareness of change.

I will be the first one to agree that initially, it will seem very difficult to start making changes in your life that put God first in everything. However, once you make the decision, you will find that living with faith and a positive attitude to change, requires as much energy and effort as living with doubt, worry, fear and uncertainty. Then, once you start trusting Him more, you realize that you can change.

For a large part of my life, although I was a Christian, I had let the ways of the world influence my thoughts, actions and words, which impacted my life plans, which made me look like everyone in this world. We do live in this world, but we should not become like this world. We need to work every day to include Him, not as an add-on, but as "The One." This doesn't mean that you won't have doubts, worries and fears, but it does mean that you can have peace and faith through your tough times. Your life does have a plan, a better plan, and there is a light at the end of the tunnel.

I know that God has always been with me, all the time. There has never been a doubt in my mind. However, I kept Him at a distance to make sure that I didn't feel too bad about my behavior. At times, when I was strong in my faith, I would let my light shine and I felt wonderful. However, when I wasn't strong, when I wasn't living right or when I was just not being happy, I would make sure that I was keeping Him at a reasonable distance. I did this, so I could still feel good about myself. As if He didn't know.

The explanation that I can give is that it was like I was walking through a very long tunnel made of glass, like at an aquarium. The tunnel represented my life's journey. I would walk down the middle of the tunnel and God was ALWAYS walking at the same pace as me, right next to me, but always on the outside of the glass. Not because He wanted to be there, but because I wouldn't let Him in. The glass allowed me to see Him and be assured of His presence, but it also served the purpose of keeping Him from being too close in my life. I wanted His presence, but not His conviction over me, primarily because I was ashamed of my actions. To others, I am also ashamed to say, that I didn't want to come across as "religious." Ironically, when I had low points in my life, I would become angry with God for not being with me. How silly was that thinking, because He was always there. It was only when I learned to become obedient and change my life, that I finally learned and made the decision to break down that glass wall. We would no longer be separated. I would welcome Him because I was no longer ashamed, and I was empowered by this new amazing and peaceful presence.

His love is unconditional. There is nothing that you have done or that you can do to mess it up. Accept this as a truth and remind yourself of this when you are feeling low. When you are down, it's easy to feel hopeless and abandoned. Just know that you are never alone and hope is always present. You only have to believe and seek.

In my new walk, following His plan, He is still with me and I can still see Him; but now I can feel, know and have a completely different kind of love with Him. There are no barriers between us. The reality is that His love has never changed. Mine has.

Most of us live our lives this same way, by using God as a convenience. Sometimes we only call on Him when we are at our darkest moments. It is a truth that no one wants to admit. This is usually apparent when we face some kind of bad or life-changing event, usually with undesirable consequences. He is always there for us, but sometimes we are only there, obediently, when we feel the need or when it is convenient for us. This mindset is counter-productive to building the kind of relationship that we need. Turning away from the ways of the world is very hard indeed.

God made you and me and He knows everything about us and everything that will happen in our lives. We have been prepared for every situation that we will encounter, even when we feel like we can't make it. He loves us unconditionally and wants us all of us, all of the time, good and bad. He wants you to call on Him when you are at your lowest, but He also asks that you praise Him at your highest and all times in between! Give thanks and praise during your good times, but also find the strength to give praise and

5

thanks during difficulties, even when you don't understand what is happening or why it is happening. Of course, this is easier said than done, but it is, in fact, your choice. During good times it's easy to give thanks, yet during difficult times it is equally important to give thanks to God. You are going through whatever it is that you are going through for a reason. He is with you and you must believe that the situation ultimately serves a purpose for His plans for your life.

Life's Standards

There is one constant in life: change will happen. Your life involves people, routines, circumstances, events and God's will. With almost all of these, you have limited power in controlling what happens. What you can control is your faith and your attitude about how you respond to what happens to you. You can also control your decision to act.

Circumstances will happen, and things will not always be in your favor; no one plans on leaving the house and getting in a wreck, but it happens. You might go into work and find out that you have suddenly been laid off, or you might get the surprise gift of a promotion. Things will happen to you, but they are not the standards in your life. They are merely events happening according to events, people, circumstances and of course, God's will.

To better explain how you should view this as you progress in life, I have created a graph. As you look at the graph, you will notice that there are three lines. These lines represent measurements, highs and lows, of where you are when events happen in your life, with examples.

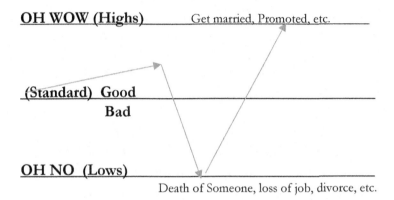

The Top Line is the "OH WOW" line. Anything from the "Good" line which is above "The Standard" line, up to this line, would measure positive events that happen in your life.

The Middle Line is the "Standard" line. This represents life as a regular day without any major events.

The Bottom Line, the "OH NO" line, represents the challenges that you face in your life. Anything from the "Bad" line down to this line measures everything negative that happens in your life.

If you have a tragic event, say a death in your family, you can see that this can drop you well below your life standard to the "OH NO" line. Likewise, if you have a major victory, like getting promoted, or getting engaged, you can be propelled up to the "OH WOW" line.

In life, you are either moving forward and up or forward and down. We don't move backwards. We simply choose to stay at certain levels depending on the circumstances that we encounter. Right now, you are probably saying, I'm not choosing to stay unhappy or mad, things have happened to me!

Yes, things may have happened, but you must learn to adjust and choose to move on. This mindset becomes more relevant when facing a difficult challenge. We might become depressed, create a negative attitude, and feel that our life is meaningless. We might even feel that we are not even capable of moving forward. This is the point where we stop living and stay low on the chart. The thought of your life being worthless is simply not true, but this is how we get in trouble; we stop living for and trusting in God's plans.

You must remember that God is always with you and He wants you to focus on serving Him! You must also believe this and say this to yourself: All things are temporary; God is in control.

During good times, we tend to recognize, rejoice and praise God when we are above the "standard" line. The challenge with this mindset is that you might get an unrealistic expectation of life and things might appear tougher when you fall again. Enjoy where you are, but understand the nature of the event that you are rejoicing in.

Remember, ALL things in life are temporary, except for God.

When we fall below the standard line, this is when we start to doubt and question God. We might even become angry. When we get to this point, sometimes we tend to stay there and hold ourselves below life's standards. We might even feel like we have the right to stay down there. We don't.

We must learn to think and believe that everything happens for a reason. A great event is simply that; a great event. It isn't permanent or the new standard in your life. Likewise, a bad event is simply that; a bad event. Neither of them becomes the new standard in your life. You will only stay at a place that you choose to stay at, and you will only stay there if you choose to stay there.

Life's events do not happen to define us, they happen to "refine" us. We must keep moving forward and we must keep moving upwards.

"God allows us to go through challenges, Not to DEFINE us, but to REFINE us."

Success

We often equate success with being happy. Please know that this isn't necessarily true. Your happiness is 100%

dependent on you, not your circumstances or things. When you consider that "things" do not carry emotion; you can determine that your emotions about "things" are really a direct result of your own conscious or subconscious decisions. If you are an unhappy person, regardless of how successful you become, or how many things you buy, you are still you, so you will probably remain unhappy.

The questions to ask yourself are:

1. How do I define success?
2. How do I define happiness?
3. How will I attain either one?

Success can and usually has different meanings to different people. It is important to find out what motivates you, what your goals are and what you were called to accomplish. You are your own unique person. God made you for and with a purpose. Sometimes situations that you are in can motivate you and can prompt you to become better. Success can and will have different meanings to different people. Some people measure success by money, others by fame and some by material possessions. However, those may not be the true measurements of success for you. If your goal is to be a better husband or wife and you have taken steps to make this happen and your family recognizes it, then you are indeed a success. If you choose to improve your life and your career, and you do, then you are successful.

Happiness

Happiness, on the other hand, is a state of mind, based on your reaction or response to something. Sometimes it might be a very difficult choice for you to be happy, especially if you are going through a hardship. Being sad and staying sad is a difficult mindset to come out of, so you must look inside of yourself, (not outside to things) to find and remember your own happiness. You can have many material things and personal relationships, but if you are not content with your own life, you will still not be happy.

Happiness is not offered by others, nor is it found in things. Buying a material possession or celebrating an event can certainly create joy, but true internal happiness is based on your decision to follow Christ.

Appreciating where you are in life and what you have materialistically, is a big start. Understand that purchasing more items does not bring true happiness. You may not live or work where you want to and that's fine, but to move to the next level, you must learn to appreciate what you have today. God will provide blessings in your life in many ways, but how can He continue to bless you with more opportunity if you cannot appreciate where you already are and what you already have?

When you understand that every situation in your life is merely a stepping stone and part of God's plan, then you start to understand the value and importance of everything in your life. Everything that you do and every situation that you encounter, is a step that must be taken in order to get to the top of the next step. When you lose the importance of a life's step due to a setback, it will keep you from moving forward and moving closer towards God's plan for your life.

There is a plan for your life, a better plan.

We are born perfect in God's eyes, fully prepared to succeed, but along the way, we lose sight of whose we are and what we're capable of achieving through trusting in Him. Life happens to us and we start engaging in bad or unhealthy things. We might begin to abuse alcohol, drugs, food or something else. We might start getting angry, depressed, or create unhealthy addictions, thoughts or actions. Sometimes we completely redefine who we think we are, due to the confusion and deception in this world. However, God's message is very clear: He has already equipped you for His plan. You just need to trust in Him, accept Him and accept who He created you to be.

When you were born, do you remember that tag made of flesh attached to your side? You know, the one that said, "addict," "depressed," "anger issues," "fearful," "worried," "confused" or something else that was negative?

No, you say? You don't remember having that or even being born with an extra flesh tag with a negative description of yourself? Of course not, because it wasn't there.

The reason it wasn't there, is because God never put it there! This is the part where you might say, but Mike, I do have a defining negative characteristic and it is a part of me, but I've always been that way! This is where I tell you that you are wrong. God never gave you any negative defining characteristics. That was all your doing.

Living in a world dominated by sin, causes us to sin. Sometimes, we can sin so much and for so long that we can get confused and accept the sin as our own identity. We can confuse what we DO, as who we are. I challenge you to accept and believe that the things you DO, really aren't who you are. I'm not talking about shirking responsibility for your actions, I am talking about separating what God made you to be, versus what you have added to your life through what you DO. If you are doing things you shouldn't be doing, stop doing them! Once you stop doing those things, you will remove from your life what you brought in or introduced. God never intended those things to be there in the first place.

Sometimes, we do negative and sinful things for so long that we can cover ourselves in those things, hiding who we truly are. When diamonds are mined from the earth, the seekers can be deceived as they sort through thick chunks of carbon. However, if they can keep their eyes on the prize, not on the nasty carbon, the seekers can and usually will find the brilliant gems inside, covered by the years of darkness. It can be difficult to sort through thick layers of dark decay.

It requires great work to remove the layers of carbon to reveal the brilliance of the beautiful diamond inside.

Our lives with Christ are similar to mining diamonds.

God has given us His brilliant, shining light to be found inside, just like a brilliant and precious diamond is found embedded with layers of black, hardened carbon. The challenge is that some of us have hidden the brilliant light within, by covering ourselves with layers of dark carbon, represented by years of sinful nature, negative actions, and habits. Some of us have been sinning for so long that we have falsely accepted the layers of carbon as a part of who we are. When we do this, we allow the layers of darkness to prevent God's brilliant light within us from shining to the rest of the world, assuming we have accepted His light: Jesus.

The great news is that although you may not feel like you can remove the years of negativity or darkness that you may be trapped in, God loves you and He can! He makes all things new! He can help you remove the years of negative and sinful things that have been hiding His light inside of you if you only trust in Him!

Yes, you and God started your life journey and it will be just you and God who will end your life journey together, if you know Him. Will you be prepared to give an account of what you did according to His plans for your life?

You can be prepared…. right now.

Here is how:

The Bible says that the only way to know God is through Jesus. In fact, Jesus said, "I am the way, the truth, and the life. No one can come to the Father except through me." John 14: 6.

This means that by asking Jesus into your life, you can know God, be forgiven of your sins and have eternal life in Heaven. In your own words, pray and repent of your sins and confess that you believe Jesus died for your sins on the cross. Acknowledge Jesus Christ as your Lord and Savior and ask Him into your heart. Tell Him you want to start new.

If you said this prayer on your own free will right now, then congratulations, you have been saved and you are fully equipped to start a better plan, God's plan! Praise God.

However, you need to continue to do your part and live your life in a way that honors God, by getting into a Christian Church that teaches about Jesus and the Bible

Now go forth and make your life exceptional!

- Mike Rodriguez

www.MikeRodriguezInternational.com

Chapter 1 – Your Life Is a Gift to You

Chapter 2

Finding My Perfect Match
By Kelli Boone

A former single mom's 3-step system to finding a healthy relationship.

All the guys I date are crazy. They are all jerks. They all act the same way. So, I guess I should just give up on dating altogether or just accept that this is what dating is supposed to look like. Mr. Right doesn't exist except in Hallmark movies.

These were the things that I told myself constantly when it came to dating. I had a belief that it wasn't me that was the problem, it was everybody else. I attracted all the wrong people in what I believed were all the right places. I was in this endless loop of constantly dating different guys with all the same characteristics and traits, therefore justifying my hypothesis that all men were the same. I felt trapped. I lost hope. Then, God showed up in the most unexpected way and turned my world upside down. Today, I want to share with you my story of how I found my way out of this endless cycle. I also want to give you strategies that you can use in your own life if you or someone you know may be going through a similar struggle. I do not claim to be an expert in relationships, however, I am an expert in how I overcame the struggles that I faced within MY relationships. I believe that many of the things that I struggled with are things that many of us struggle with and I firmly believe that God does not bring us through the valley to the mountaintop to stand still. He calls us to share those victories with the rest of the world. Psalm 105:2 states, "Sing to him; Yes, Sing his praises. Tell everyone about his wonderful deeds" and serves as a great reminder that we are called to share the great things that God has done in our lives. God calls us to be his disciples. He calls us to do his work on this earth. I pray that you find these strategies to be a helpful tool in your own journey to finding a healthy relationship.

It all began while I was in high school. I was surrounded with many examples of what I believed a relationship was supposed to look like. What I did not realize at the time was that many of these relationships were unhealthy. They involved yelling, fighting, verbal abuse, mental abuse, coping with the use of alcohol and drugs, and violence. This was all I knew at the time and I did not know that my perception of relationships was not right. Therefore, I found myself in relationship after relationship where I was either treated badly, or if I was in a good relationship, I would find a way to ruin it out of fear of it turning bad like my other relationships. I was unaware that there was a problem with any of my relationships because I did not know, at the time, what was possible. I had no clue that I had the power to find someone that would treat me with respect. Most importantly, I did not know that in order to have a healthy relationship with someone else, you first have to have a healthy relationship with God, and then yourself. You have to respect yourself enough to know what you do and do not deserve in any relationship. You also have to have some key things in place in order to successfully move forward in the right direction to find the person that God has created for you. I want to share three things that I have found to be the most helpful in my life that created lasting change and helped me begin to move forward in finding a healthy, lasting relationship. By doing these three things, I went from being a single mother who struggled for many years to find Mr. Right, to a happily married woman who found a good man who was exactly what she was looking for. Now, I want to help those who struggle with the same thing to get out of the endless cycle and begin to see what it can be like to have lasting love. In the next few paragraphs, I am going to cover in detail why these three things are absolutely imperative to have as your core foundation in every relationship in order to make it successful.

Here are some things that really made the difference in helping me to find the right relationship:

1. God
2. Experts
3. Certainty

GOD

In order for you to be able to find a healthy relationship, you have to have some things in place before you can see your desired result. The one thing that I believe is the most important to have established first is having God as your rock and your foundation in your life. If you have God at the center of your life, you are no longer being influenced by society's views of what a relationship is supposed to look like. Instead, you are looking deeper and relying on God, who shows you infinite love and what a real loving relationship is supposed to look like, if you will let him. But, that also requires us to listen to him and follow, even if we don't understand why.

In my own life, the thing that God asked me to do was to stop dating, take time to be near Him, get to know Him, and be happy with myself. This was extremely tough for me because I was co-dependent in all of my relationships until that point. What this meant was that I relied on the person that I was dating to be the influence of who I was supposed to be, and essentially, I was never myself in any relationship, which explained my constant stress and unhappiness. I would find myself putting all of my focus and energy in wanting the person I was dating to achieve their goals, which did not exist, instead of accomplishing my own goals, which did exist. I would put my goals on the backburner because I was more focused on how I could fit myself into that person's life goals instead of having independent goals that I should have been working on to better myself. I didn't understand why God needed me to be alone, but I followed his request anyway. During this time alone, I learned that God loved me for who I was and that I did not have to act like anyone other than myself to earn his love. I learned that God valued me, that he loved me regardless of the flaws that I disliked about myself. I learned to love myself for who I was and not settle for anything less than someone who respected and loved me for the same reasons. I no longer felt the need to act like someone I wasn't to impress guys who didn't respect me in the first place. I was finally happy with the person I was because I knew that as long as God loved me, he would bring me the right person when HIS timing was right and when he knew I was ready. But, I had to be content in the waiting, patient in the process, and let God be involved in ALL of my decisions. In order to make sure I made God my priority, this required me to fully immerse my life in learning as much as I could about God and include God in my life daily. This was what lead me to the next step in my journey with God, letting HIM show me the way.

After hitting rock bottom in the relationship department over and over, I decided that it was time to focus on the one relationship that I believed could have the biggest impact of positive change in my life: my relationship with God. I believed this because I always heard people at my church talk about the miracles God did in their own lives. I always heard about how good God's intentions were to help us in our lives. I just did not believe that he wanted those things for me, personally. I went to church when I was younger and knew a little about God, but I never really invested a lot of time into getting to know him and developing a relationship with him. I did not know what that looked like. How do you have a relationship with someone you can't even see? How do you hear and talk to him? How do you know he is there? How do you know he is listening? All these questions ran through my mind as I was debating on where to start and how. So, I did the one thing I knew how to do and prayed. I asked God to help me see where I needed to start. That's when I heard something on the radio that I had never heard before. I drive a company car, which happens to be a different car every day, so the stations are usually random stations I never listen to that I have to reprogram once I get into the car. However, this station was different and it was exactly where I needed to start that day. It was a Christian radio station that was having a 30-day challenge. They encouraged everyone who was seeking to get closer to the Lord to listen to that station only for 30 days and see how God began to work in their lives. I had not listened to Christian music a lot prior to this moment, so I decided to give it a try for 30 days and see if it actually worked. It was the start of doing something very imperative to developing my journey with God, opening my heart to receive the words of God through music. The first immediate change I noticed was that my mood was better. I felt empowered. It encouraged me to pray and ask God for guidance about everything in my life. I looked forward to hearing God's messages being spoken through the people on this station. Then, it inspired me to continue my journey of including God in my life more and get involved with learning more about God through Bible studies.

Our church had a women's Bible study every Tuesday and I made this a priority to attend every week. These Bible studies have allowed me to grow deeper into God's Word and learn more about his intentions and how Jesus lived his life. They also gave me an inside look at exactly how much he loved me. Through those Bible studies, I learned how to live a life that honored God. Some of the things that I do now include:

1. Surrounding myself with biblical women
2. Listening to Christian music
3. Reading the Bible

4. Growing deeper with God through Bible studies
5. Developing a closer relationship with God through prayer

I also learned that, at that time, I was not living a life that honored God. I spent my free time going out with friends, having a few drinks, then meeting guys who looked attractive on the outside, but on the inside had motives that were not for my best interest. I failed to notice those characteristics in the guys I would meet before getting close to God. In fact, I did not see myself as worthy of receiving love from a good guy. However, now that God was in my proximity, I began to question whether the things I was doing were honoring him. I began to develop characteristics that were like his and I began to change the way I was living my life.

This is the power of proximity. You become most like the people you surround yourself with, and in my case, it changed the way I looked at relationships. It helped me see that I was not meeting people in the right environment. I was meeting people that were NOT doing things that honored God. I was one of those people who was not honoring God. Therefore, I attracted other people who were not honoring God. You attract what you are. In order to change the type of people that you attract, you first have to change YOU, then what you will accept in your life moving forward. Once you decide what you will no longer accept in your life, you will begin to weed out the people that God never intended for you to have in your life to begin with. My proximity to God helped me realize what I deserved to have in my relationships. Then, I began to realize that I needed some other people to help me along my journey with God: EXPERTS.

EXPERTS

I spent a good majority of my life feeling intimidated to admit that I did not know everything. I was embarrassed to ask people for help. I thought I was supposed to somehow figure things out on my own. I didn't want to be that person who had all those problems and couldn't deal with them. However, after getting out of another bad relationship and knowing that if I continued this pattern, I would never be able to show my son what a good, healthy relationship was supposed to look like, I decided that it was time to ask for help. This was when my eyes were opened to the importance of experts.

What I didn't realize was that most experts have already been down a similar road and figured out what works and what doesn't. They have made the mistakes already. They have struggled. But, they have figured out a way to come out on top. The biggest perk for you is that by talking with those experts, they can help you come out on top much faster, essentially allowing you to quickly find a solution to your problem. They also remind you that you are not alone in your struggles and there is a way to work through them. Plus, they will hold you accountable to make sure you stay on the right track. The first expert I decided to seek was my faith-based counselor.

I remember my first-day meeting with her. I began by telling her about my relationship struggles, the struggles of being a single mother, and my struggles with my relationship with

God. She had also been a single mother at one point who was in an unhealthy relationship, but she figured out how to find a good relationship using God as a tool. She began to describe to me what a healthy relationship was supposed to look like. It involved always having God as the center of your focus, not the person you are dating. It involved you being independently motivated to do the things that God calls you to do, but coming together with your partner to move towards your individual calling. It involved dating a guy that loves God first and that focuses on God first. It means that you both independently love God more than each other. You put God in the center of your world, always. You go to God for everything, always. Then, you come together to work towards the things God has called you to do. But, you always make God your center, no one else. She began to give me a vision for myself that I never knew was possible. She began to help me see what I had been missing in all of my relationships until that point: my belief in my self-worth. I didn't believe that I was worthy of receiving love from a good man because I focused on that person to give me what God wanted to give me all along, his acceptance and love. I was so caught up in finding someone that I thought was attractive on the outside that I would overlook their low moral character on the inside. I was more focused on finding someone that the world would view as perfect instead of the right person that God created specifically for me. However, by going to my faith-based counselor, I began to see what I needed to begin to focus on immediately, making God the center of my world. Once I began to make God my central focus, I began to have confidence in myself again and continued to pursue the final thing that I believe helped me find the right relationship, certainty.

CERTAINTY

I never understood the power of certainty until I attended Tony Robbins' *Unleash the Power Within* conference. At this conference, I learned how to take control of the things that I wanted in my life and to demand the results I wanted from MYSELF. I realized that by having certainty about what I wanted, I knew exactly what to focus on to get it, and therefore I found ways to attract the things into my life that helped me achieve my goals. I also learned that goal setting does not always have to be for your financial or work goals. You can also set goals for your relationships.

I began this exercise by writing down exactly what I would want the man I marry to be like. I described in detail what standards he would hold for himself, what we both would like to do together, what our family would be like, how he would treat my son, and how we would continue to grow our relationship each year. I made a list of qualities that I would love to have in my significant other and non-negotiables that I no longer wanted. This was how I described my perfect man.

MY IDEAL MAN WOULD:

My ideal man would love God first. He would be excited to seek the things of God. He would be a leader for our family. He would be courageous. He would be a loving step-parent to my son. He would be a role model and someone I would want my son to look up to and respect as he grows older. He would be a great listener. He would be patient. He would love to hike. He would love to run. He would be adventurous and spontaneous. He would value his health and continuously work on bettering our marriage.

MY IDEAL MAN WOULD NOT:

My ideal man would not drink, smoke, or seek the party lifestyle. He would not yell at me when he is frustrated. He would not treat my son as if he was not valued. He would not engage in things that create an unhealthy lifestyle. He would not put God on the backburner. He would not be a negative person. He would not treat me badly in our relationship. He would not make me feel insignificant in his life or my own life for mistakes I make along the way.

What I did after I wrote down what my ideal husband would look like was the biggest key to helping me break the pattern in my life of finding the wrong people. I MADE A DECISION TO NO LONGER ACCEPT THE WOULD-NOT'S IN ANY OF MY RELATIONSHIPS. The "would-not" list that I created was the new standard that I began to hold for anyone that I met who could be on my dating radar. When I decided to be absolutely clear about what I would no longer accept, I began to weed out all of the people that God did not intend to have in my life. I began to notice when a guy had the qualities I was looking for and walk away from the guys who did not. I began to feel empowered and have confidence in myself. For the first time in my life, I knew exactly what my expectations were in any relationship that I would have moving forward. I stopped being afraid to stand up for myself, my standards, and what I deserved to have in a relationship. I started being CERTAIN about what I wanted and I MADE A DECISION to make it happen in my life.

I followed God, found experts to influence and help me get along further, and became CERTAIN about what I would no longer accept in my life. As a result, I found my journey with God taking me on my first mission trip to Costa Rica. I was a single mom struggling to find Mr. Right. I had gotten out of yet another bad relationship a few months prior. I followed God's requests. I took time alone. I found myself. I began to learn how to be happy with myself for the first time in my life. I was certain about what I wanted in a relationship, but patient in God's process of waiting. I distracted myself from thinking about the fact that I was single and focused on the things that I enjoyed doing in my life. I decided to take a break from the dating world and went to Costa Rica on my first mission trip to serve God. While I was there, I found someone in the most unlikely place, in the most unlikely circumstance, and the most unexpected way, my husband. In order for me to be the person God needed me to be for him, I needed that time alone to find out who I was in God. I needed the knowledge from the experts I surrounded myself with to teach me what a healthy relationship was supposed to look like. I needed clarity and certainty on exactly what I was looking for. Then, I needed to keep my eyes open and wait for God to finish doing his work in me so I could be ready when Mr. Right found me.

My husband will forever walk alongside me serving God, leading our family, and constantly looking for ways to make me happy. He is exactly what I was looking for in a spouse because I had written down what I wanted and prayed for him before I met him. If you are in that place in your life where you have not found what you are looking for in a relationship, I would encourage you to evaluate where you stand in these three categories. What will you no longer accept in a relationship? What will you demand to have in a relationship? Most importantly, what will you begin to work towards to attract the right people? Our actions are a direct result of what we will get out of life. By doing nothing to change your situation, you are only prolonging the time that it will take to find the right person. I spent years of my life going in endless circles, following the same patterns, and yielding the same result of attracting the wrong people. God, experts, and certainty changed everything for me. Now, let me ask you, are you going to continue the same unhealthy patterns in your relationships, or are you going to take control of your life and do something about it?

As I close out this chapter, I want to ask you a few questions. Grab a pen and paper because I want you to write down your answers to these questions. I want you to ponder your answers and think about how you could begin working today towards finding the right relationship for you.

1. Are you standing in the way of God's intentions for your ideal relationship or are you letting God lead the way?

2. What experts are you reaching out to or could you begin to reach out to help you get further along in your journey?

3. What are the "would-not's" that you will decide not to stand for in any relationship?

If you find these strategies to be helpful to you, would you share this book with other people? Then, together, we can change the world, one relationship at a time.

If you enjoyed reading this chapter, you would enjoy reading my full book, *"Beyond Limits"* which is available to purchase on Amazon or Barnes & Noble.

About the Author – Kelli Boone

Kelli Boone is a full-time Sales professional, Mother, Wife, and follower of Christ. She has climbed up the corporate ladder, landing herself in the top 10% in the country, as a single mother for half of her career. She strives to show the world that you can have success and maintain a healthy balance with your family. She is also passionate about helping those who struggle to find a healthy relationship, as this was a big hurdle that once she figured out how to get past, created a trickle-down effect that brought huge success in other areas in her life, hence, creating the overall success that she had been looking for all along. She now seeks to teach others who find themselves in that place where they feel like they are in an endless loop of attracting the wrong people to know exactly what it is that they need to have in place to find a lasting relationship. She believes that if you get your relationships right, everything else in your life will succeed as a result, and looks forward to providing you with the strategies you need to break through and demand the best for yourself.

She can be reached at www.kelliboone.com

Chapter 2 – Finding My Perfect Match

Chapter 3

Let God Be Your Tomorrow
By Fred Kienle

As I sang these words: *"Let the Devil take tomorrow, Lord tonight I need a friend..."* I could feel an uneasy and chilling sense of dread wash over my conscience.

I had been a musician for over 23 years and sang those words, and words like them, many times before... but lately, it just didn't seem right. It's nice to be popular in a local well-known band because of the accolades and attention that made you feel important. These were always a welcome feeling. For 14 years we performed weekly in one of the most popular night clubs in El Paso, TX. The group had been on tour to cities like Denver, Co and Chicago, IL. We had a #4 song on the local hit radio charts. At one time, we even fronted for a *Gary Puckett and the Union Gap* concert. We had a solid reputation and a comfortable following of fans. Sitting down with the customers on the breaks was always an exciting feeling. They would stroke your ego and tell you how wonderful the group sounded and how much fun they were having.

Being in the club life four nights a week was always an open temptation for Satan to influence you, with people offering you all kinds of drugs and other tantalizing items. By the Grace of GOD, I never got into drugs, but I did smoke cigarettes a lot and managed to down at least two scotch on the rocks every night. Friday and Saturday nights were exceptionally rough because everyone wanted to buy the band a round of tequila shots and were highly insulted if you refused. You couldn't drink them all, so by the end of the evening you would find several shot glasses full of tequila sitting behind our amplifiers and equipment. My father was an alcoholic and I always had a fear of becoming one myself. Fortunately, through God's mercy, I never did. However, there were nights that I should have never gotten behind the wheel of my car and driven home. I know to this day that God placed a guardian angel in the passenger seat when I did drive home those nights. In my heart I knew I was a Christian and believed that Jesus was my Lord and Savior. I even read the Bible on occasion, but only in a passive manner. I often prayed about being a better person and in the early 80's a sense of conviction began slowly entering my heart.

I mentioned earlier that sitting down with the customers was always a good feeling… well, that feeling began to fade. In the past, I would ask them, "Hey! How are you all doing tonight?" and they would always reply, "Great!" The conversation would always be light, full of compliments and laughter. But recently, it seemed I was prompted to dig a little deeper and seriously ask things like, "No, I mean, how are things really going, and is everything alright at home or at work?" Oh boy, talk about a 180 degree turn around.

That's when the TRUE person would emerge and begin to tell you some of the sad and unfortunate things that were going on in their lives. I began to understand that so many, in fact, too many people going out to the clubs were not going out to have fun, but to HIDE and drink themselves away from their own reality. So, it was just as important to them for me, being the popular band guy, to stroke their egos and feelings as it was for them to stroke mine. This was a paradigm shift in the making. That's when my heart began to have a totally different connection to the people I was performing for.

One evening as I sang those words, GOD opened my eyes and I could see Satan and his demonic angels touching many of the souls out on the dance floor, whispering in their ears, "Go ahead, it's alright, listen to what he is saying, do what the song says, let ME take tomorrow and you can sin tonight… It's OK!" I knew then and there, the words to many of the songs we sang were subliminally encouraging some of these confused souls to do the wrong things. You have heard the saying, "Hung by the tongue," haven't you? Well, I felt like I was "Hung by the tongue that sung!" We all know the spoken word, good or bad, has an incredible amount of power, and GOD was showing me the words that were coming from myself when I sang had the same impact on others as well as myself. As I sang these songs, I began to feel like I was throwing poisoned darts at these unsuspecting souls. I was guilty of giving Satan another avenue to weave his evil thoughts into their hearts. It wasn't long after these convictions began to invade my heart and soul that I decided that it was time to make a tremendous change. I had started this band back in 1963 and had nourished and led it up until this time. I know that GOD was encouraging me to hang this part of my life up and head a different direction in my future. This was a little scary because my music was my passion. I would ask God on a daily basis, "Hey! If I give this up, what's next???" All I heard was silence and there was no forthcoming answer. So, all I could do was put my trust in Him and have enough faith to realize that as He closes one door, He will always open another one. So, now begins a new adventure in my life!

I have always been an entrepreneur, and besides being a musician and playing in the band, I had started a small business of installing electrical controls for new types of solar water heaters, room heaters, and pool heaters. I was going and blowing and doing a fair business when the bottom began to drop out of the market. Construction was diminishing and steady work was hard to come by. My wife and I prayed for a solution to this problem and still did not know what to do. This was around the same time that GOD was dealing with the songs I was singing and the effect it was having on others. We began to realize that El Paso was not a place for us and our daughter to really grow in. The question was, where do we go? After many prayers and talks with God... things started becoming visible as tangible possibilities.

My uncle had recently moved from El Paso to the Dallas area to open a new school supply store. I asked him how the job opportunities were down there and he said he knew a guy in the HR Department at a major semiconductor corporation, which began a new 'God-Planned Sequence of

Events' for me and my family. I called this friend of my uncle and he asked me to come down for an interview. I packed a few things and after my wife and I prayed over this new possibility, I climbed into my 1972 Chevy El Camino and headed for Dallas. I was excited at the prospect of a new beginning and new place to start over again. However, I still had some trepidation and fear of leaving my comfort zone and all the things that I grew up with. The interview went very well and they wanted to hire me, but there was no opening at the present time. You know the old saying, "Don't call us, we'll call you." My heart sank a little and I thought, 'Maybe God is showing me this is not the right road I should take.'

I stayed in Dallas for another week looking through the newspapers for any other possibilities with no real luck. Just about the time I was deciding to go back to El Paso, I got a call from my uncle's friend and he asked me to come back in for another interview. I was excited and prayed heavily about this visit. "Please God, if this is right, let it happen." My faith and patience were paying off. Here is where God's favor started to work in my direction. One of the employees, who I found out later was a devout Christian, had been praying about a much higher position, and guess what? God opened this door for him, which opened the door for me to step into his place and secure a really nice job. "Patience, patience, patience… it's all in God's timing," I kept telling myself.

The other employee's new position was not available for several weeks. I had already been out of work for a while and this left me financially stranded for yet another stretch of undetermined time. Ouch! Well expense-wise, I couldn't stay in Dallas and wait until these things fell into place, so I packed up and headed back to El Paso. I was home one day when God stepped in again with HIS plan. I received a call from a general construction company that did contract work for the major company I had interviewed with. He said that the person in HR called him and asked if there was a possibility of temporarily hiring me until their position opened up. And there it was... how about that for a 'touch from God'! Well, the next day I was on the road back to Dallas with a job in hand. It seemed like a huge burden had been lifted from my shoulders. All the worry and fretting I had been doing was a wasted effort. I had asked God for His help and if I would have just relaxed and let Him work His plan, I would have saved myself a lot of unnecessary grief.

Now the pressure was off because God had supplied me with a temporary job that would sustain us until the main employment began. This all happened quite rapidly and it was great, but all kinds of other issues began to come into focus. What do I do with our house in El Paso and where do we live in Dallas? While I was in Dallas working, my wife and daughter were left with the challenge of packing and getting our house ready for sale. We prayed together several times over the phone, asking for guidance and direction. I remember at one time a pastor had told me that when you're not quite sure of what to pray for, just say this, "GOD...HELP!" And help HE did. Soon afterwards, we heard of a guy that was buying homes to resell. He came over and offered us a fair price to buy our home outright, plus pay the closing costs. One problem down and one more to go.

While this was going on, I was frantically looking for a nice place for us to live that was close enough to where I would be working. I was only looking for a place to rent until we became established and could spend some quality time finding a home to buy. All of the rental properties that I looked at were really run down and not right. I had gone to several real estate establishments on the off chance they could steer me in the right direction. One of the ladies at one real estate office knew of a family that wanted to rent their home and gave me their number. It was the right house, the right price, and close enough to my work. It was also close to a good school for our daughter to attend. I believe that we received another 'touch from God'! Now all we had to do was MOVE. Things happened really fast then. My wife meticulously packed all of our belongings, I came home for the weekend, rented a large U-Haul, we packed it to the hilt, said our goodbyes to everyone, and off we went to become "Dallasites" with a brand-new future in front of us.

It wasn't long after we moved when the position I applied for opened up and I transferred into my permanent job. Wow, what a comforting feeling to realize that God's plan placed me into a position where I was fully employed, with a company that offered me and my family stability, benefits, and opportunity.

The first supervisor I reported to was a blessing; he was such a good-natured fellow, he trusted me, and he allowed me to be creative in my work. He would put me in charge of special projects that made my efforts very visible to others in the company. Because of this, I was sent to another building that did a lot of research and development.

I was classified as a Lead Electrician and my salary increased. Yippie! My supervisor there was also one of the good guys and soon I was working on some very interesting laboratories installing some very intricate and delicate equipment for some very interesting PhD's. You think GOD had a hand in all this? I know He did! After a few years in that position I had become a team leader and was in charge of the nine men in the crew. At that time, my supervisor had some health issues and was going to be out for quite some time. However, instead of getting a new supervisor, the facilities manager at the time just let me continue to work with the crew and leave everything status quo. I didn't mind and was quite happy doing my job. The company was very good at offering training to the employees and I wanted to learn more about using computers. Computer training was the only thing I felt that I was held back on. My facilities manager said that I only needed to involve myself in the training pertaining to my field of work. That was a bummer.

Patience paid off again. The existing facilities manager moved to another position and was replaced. Here is where another blessing was handed to me because the new guy was not just a manager, he was a true leader. He immediately promoted me to a supervisor position and left me in charge of the R&D building crew. My salary increased again! And guess what? He didn't understand why I was not allowed to take any of the computer classes and gave me permission to attend a lot of PC training. This helped open up new direction and opportunities.

I have always been blessed with a happy and positive attitude. People would, and will, always ask me how I stay so positive and upbeat. My answer has always been the same, "I had nothing to do with it, it's a gift from God!" I believe that because of my attitude I was moved from the R&D building back to the main building to become a project manager. I also attended many of the all-day positive attitude seminars that featured world-known motivational speakers like Zig Ziglar, Anthony Robbins, Tom Blanchard, and so many others. I felt a growing passion deep down inside of me to be able to speak like that and help other people.

I became involved with other departments and one in particular was the Environmental Health and Safety (EH&S) department. They noticed how I was conducting the safety meeting for my team and asked if I would like to teach some of their safety classes. Being the ham that I am, I jumped at the opportunity. You know, as a musician I loved being on stage, and to be able to teach some folks to be safer was a welcomed use of my talent and passion.

It seemed that every large company had some "flavor of the month" type of new progress program. Things like "The Circle of Quality," "The Wheel of Excellence," etc. These were fanned out to all the employees as a process to have them participate in the growth of the company. These programs would flourish for a few months, then slowly disappear into oblivion. However, one program began to emerge that seemed to have some real merit and quality to it. It was called Six Sigma and is still being used today. I eagerly signed up for one of the first "Six Sigma Specialist" training classes. It lasted only 2 days and I wanted more. I talked to one of the trainers and he liked my attitude and suggested that I ask my boss if I could become a candidate as a "Six

Sigma Expert." It turned out that an engineer in our group was also interested in this program. His qualifications and status made him a better choice for the position. This other person was a friend of mine and I knew he would be a good fit for the position and do it well. I figured that God had another plan for me to pursue and relied on my faith in HIM for my next step. Guess what? This engineer accepted a job offer at another company that he had been praying about. This opened the door for me to become the "Six Sigma Expert" for our department. For the next four years I trained our employees as a Six Sigma Specialist and guided their special projects. This position was quite a challenge and a terrific learning curve for me. The knowledge I gained in those four years was incredible.

After four years the company wanted the experts to return back to the regular workforce and pursue other avenues. I really didn't want to return to my former position as a project manager and, 'voila,' another door was opened. I was offered the opportunity to be the Records Retention Manager for our North Texas area. This was a whole new kettle of fish for me. I loved it because I was still in the teaching and training mode and responsible for a new group of folks.

My employment lasted over 22 years and was a blessing for me and my family. I was stretched and challenged in so many ways. Throughout those years it seemed that GOD had touched each phase of my career, opening so many doors, allowing me to grow in so many ways. It made me wonder what HE had planned for the next steps in my life.

The next phase of my career really surprised me and it started in 2014. I have always wanted to write a book and get it published, but really didn't know what to write about. I also knew that getting a book published was a real shot in the dark.

Let me explain this strange sequence of events that began to evolve in my life.

At a drive-through of a local fast food restaurant, I calmly spoke my order into the squawk box and I sensed that the young man at the other end was not really paying attention. I drove up to the pick-up window, paid my bill, and received my order, but before I drove away, I checked the bag and the order was all wrong. I was a little upset because this seemed to happen too often at several of these restaurants. The young man dispassionately apologized and went about fixing the mistake. As I drove away, I thought to myself, 'What is wrong with these kids? They don't seem to care or understand how important some common-sense people skills can be.' Right then and there, something happened that I will never forget. I felt GOD touch me on the shoulder and quietly say to me, *"Why don't you do something about it?"* I was dumbfounded and responded in a quivering voice with, "Like what…?" HE answered quietly, *"With all your training and attitude, teach them!"* Chills ran all over my body as I sat there thinking about the implications of what I had just experienced. 'OK. How do I accomplish this challenge?' I asked myself. As I really thought about these young folks that worked in these first-time jobs, I realized they were all good kids. Sadly enough, they were just not being taught these skills, not at home, not at school, and definitely not at work. I wondered if I could write a book on the subject of people skills to make a difference, and over the next several months, I launched myself into researching and studying the subject of people skills. I reached out to anyone I could for advice and when I found out that Zig Ziglar's office was in Dallas, I thought, 'Why not?' and boldly called them. I was not able to have a meeting with Zig Ziglar, but his gracious assistant, Laurie Magers, set me up with a meeting with a person that has become one of my mentors, Bryan Flanagan. Since this meeting, the wonderful people at the Ziglar company have become close and important friends to me. The advice I received from Bryan set me on a new course that led me to creating a seminar out of the people skills train of thought, called "Success with an Attitude." The feedback I received after delivering several of these seminars helped me develop it into a published book with the same title and a forward written by Tom Ziglar, the proud son of Zig Ziglar.

After 22 years, the company offered me an early retirement package. This was a little scary and exciting at the same time. Being unemployed did give me more time and after my book was published, it paved the way for another teaching passion I had on the subject of safety. Many of the safety training sessions I had encountered and even taught were the most boring, ineffective, and a waste of time imaginable. So, since my passion is about attitude, I designed a special seminar titled, "Safety with an Attitude." I have had great success with it and have presented it to several major corporations, cities, churches, small and large businesses, etc.

Well, God didn't stop there. As I have become a little older I have become increasingly aware of how important a person's health is to their everyday life. I also noticed that too many people, young and old, have an uneducated attitude about health. By that, I mean they are not 'verbally' active in staying healthy or recovering from an illness. I would listen to folks saying things like, "Well, it's flu season again, I'll probably get it. I get it every year!" Woah, now! Proverbs 18:21 says, *'death and life are in the power of the tongue.'* It seems like this kind of verbal abuse would open a door for Satan to step in and give a person the flu. So once again, another door was opened and a new avenue of reaching out and helping others presented itself. I designed a new seminar, "Health with an Attitude." Not only did God give me the idea, but He provided me an incredible and receptive audience in the retirement community. I never knew there were so many assisted living and retirement homes in every city and town. There are hundreds of them. It has been a delightful and fulfilling experience to be able to entertain and inspire these folks by motivating them to become aware of how important their attitude is toward health and healing.

Please remember, GOD will not forget your dreams and if you let HIM, HE will guide you into your destiny. He has allowed me to publish a book, become a motivational speaker helping others, and He is allowing me to share my story with you in this faith-filled collection. It is an honor to be included with these very talented co-authors lead by Mike Rodriguez.

Closing Thoughts

If you are going to a club to have a fun night out and are secure in yourself and your walk with the Lord, enjoy. However, if you are going there night after night to hide your problems, you might consider having a real long conversation with God and do a lot of praying over the reasons you are hiding. If you are a musician and are singing some of the songs with hurtful and hateful words, please think about what your audience and you are hearing. You don't have to give up your passion, but it would be wonderful if you discarded some of the lyrics you were singing.

My life has been an incredible journey and as I reflect back on the entire picture, it all makes sense. GOD has a plan for all of us. All we need to do is to put our trust and faith in HIM. As you read this story, I hope you realize that my life has not been a smooth ride. There have been many obstacles and pitfalls. I have made numerous mistakes and some incredibly bad choices and decisions along the way. I can only say that God's grace, mercy and love have given me the strength to go through those valleys and shadows. He has shown me how important the "spoken word" is and how to incorporate it into all my training and seminars.

HE has taken me from singing the words,

"Let the Devil take tomorrow,"

to

"Let GOD be your tomorrow."

About the Author – Fred D. Kienle

I have come up through the ranks learning how to deal with people and personalities through trial and error...! I attended Texas Western College in El Paso, Texas. I was a Musician/Recording Artist for 25 Years. My group has been on tour and an opening act for several mainline entertainers. As a Licensed Electrician, I owned several successful small businesses in El Paso. After moving to the Dallas area, I worked for a major semiconductor corporation for over 22 years as a supervisor and project manager, teaching and training hundreds of employees in Six Sigma, Ethics & Safety. I am a Certified Six Sigma Expert specializing in Team Building and Team Facilitation. I am a Licensed Health Insurance Agent, helping people by guiding them through the insurance jungle. I am a successful Writer/Author of _Success with an Attitude_, with the forward written by _Tom Ziglar the Proud Son of Zig Ziglar_. I currently conduct Success, Safety and Health Seminars for numerous cities, churches, schools, corporations and organizations throughout the Dallas/Fort Worth Metroplex. My "Health with an Attitude" seminars have become popular with our wonderful senior population in the assisted living and retirement homes. I love telling stories and I insert a lot of humor and comedy into my seminars. I am honored to be a Co-Author in this book. My approach to everything I do, always focuses on having a positive attitude and my Faith in God. I reside in Dallas with my wife of 47 years and our two dogs.

You can contact me at: fkienle@aol.com

Chapter 4

A Striving Soul Finds Freedom
By Cheneil Torbert

Dear Striving Soul,

I hear you, my soul connects with you, my life has been you.

Growing up as a competitive athlete where sports activities consumed most of my childhood, there was not much time for reflection or even appreciation, but a tendency to perform and compare. Not to be better than other people, but to rise up and make myself feel better as an attempt to overshadow insecurities. This started at a young age.

I wanted to do well and as an athlete it was easier because things like reading and understanding and tests were extremely difficult for me. I struggled a lot academically and I remember starting to label myself as being slower, "dumb," and not understanding like others early on. Something was wrong with me.

Physically, although a muscular build and athletic, I always saw myself as "bigger and fat" very early on. I vividly remember class photos where I was more than a foot taller than the entire class and this made me feel very ashamed and not pretty. I was not good enough or pretty enough or thin enough. "No wonder I can't make cheerleader, or be included with certain groups," I thought. Even in the 5th

grade, I started to believe lies. Lies about my abilities, my God-given talents, the way he made me physically.

Little did I know, these lies were seeds that Satan had begun to plant in my head that he would taunt me with for the first few decades of my life.

I learned to overcompensate these feelings of insecurity and what I thought to be my reality with trying harder, putting out more effort than most, and performing in hopes to earn a better grade or to appear to be the better athlete because I hustled harder. This would also help me hide the feelings of being challenged, dumb, fat, and unattractive compared to the other girls.

Performing allowed me to feel good about myself for a long time and my busy life was honestly a blessing because I didn't have time to think much about my feelings or care about a lot. It kept me from getting into trouble or using bad choices or relationships as a way to deal. So, a lot of the time, I was good, I was happy, but I lived under a dark cloud of insecurities, just feeling like I needed to perform better constantly.

I remember thinking on numerous occasions things like, "That's great that I scored more points in a basketball game than most in the district, or hit it over the fence in softball games most games, or earning a trip to perform at the Pro Bowl in Hawaii my senior year in high school, but… is that enough, is that good enough? I won't be as thin as the other cheerleaders when I go to Hawaii and will I be embarrassed to wear the outfit? I may have done well as an athlete in high school, but no way can I get into college playing sports, I am not suitable for that kind of thing." Somehow, I still didn't feel like I was good enough, no matter how many rewards, awards, or recognitions. Naturally, my heart wanted to prove myself wrong and do more to somehow feel better, less insecure, valuable.

I love people and had many friend groups, but often didn't even understand my place except that I enjoyed being involved. I remember a dear friend in high school telling me, "When I look at you in the crowd of all your many friend groups, I see this flicker of light in the darkness." I'll never forget it and God used this so profoundly so many years later to reveal His truth and plan to me.

But the striving continued.

Although it was unaffordable, after high school God pointed me to a private Baptist college where, much to my surprise, I was not much different than most of the other students. We were all good kids, who worked hard. I had decided not to play collegiate softball because I didn't want to add another year of debt, so instead I joined the cheerleading team, but it wasn't as competitive as I was used to. I have to admit, I felt a little lost. What could I strive for? What could I do to make myself feel productive, proud, different?

School continued to be extremely difficult in college, but by the grace of God, I was admitted into nursing school. Nursing interested me because I do love people and would consider myself having God-given servant leadership qualities, and quite frankly, I wanted to make an impact and to have a different lifestyle for my future financially. Nursing seemed to be the perfect route to take, plus it would make me feel good to care for others.

I never imagined how difficult it would be. All of the hoops of so many hours studying and failed tests and classes retaken that would be ahead of me. Not to mention the tears and begging, prayers, not only from myself but also from many like my mom and her friends on a monthly basis when I was gearing up for another exam. During school, I was no longer able to out hustle my reality. It was either pass or fail. Early on in my college career is when the lies were quickly becoming my reality and started to define me. I began to say, "You really are dumb, you can't even pass this simple class. You don't deserve to be a nurse because clearly you aren't smart enough. You really are fat, everyone else looks so much better in their uniform. You really aren't and won't be who you want to be." I began to start believing lies.

Although high school and college have different memories for many people, for me, most of my memories were good, but so hard on many levels. There were things I didn't even realize I was battling emotionally that I started to face.

God is sovereign – God protected me from so much heartache and confusion in high school, especially in relationships, and I am so grateful. Although college was super difficult, God brought me a wonderful life partner, my groom, to which I say, "Thank you, Jesus," for this gift every day. I know, He is why I ended up at a small Baptist college in East Texas and he endured all those hardships with me and today I would say meeting Him was worth it all!

God is gracious – God spared me a lot in grade school. Even though some of my decisions were not of good character, He was gracious. Amongst many other challenging things, the gravity of debt that would be owed AFTER all the struggle and the nursing degree would be a long-term chain that would impact me. It taught me about being noble with my money because it is all His, but it also showed me how

God can use things like debt to show His mercy. I consider this debt, along with the other difficult challenges, to be a learning tool God wanted to use for years to come.

God is the only way – At the end of the four years and a nursing degree later, there was still a moment of, "Is that it? I barely survived and YES, it is a great accomplishment, but is that it? Did I do enough? Can I be proud? Even though I am in a lot of debt with a great degree, will my parents be proud? Will God approve of me and my efforts? Can I do better?" There was still the desire to perform, so at this point, I was hoping marriage, landing an awesome nursing job, or who knows what, would maybe fill this "perfection power" I felt needed to be filled.

As my next season of life began to unfold, I started to toss around the idea of getting my advanced practice degree. You know, to keep up with my striving efforts and of course to challenge myself and serve others in a more gratifying and independent way. The ironic thing is, my husband was on the same page of me getting this advanced degree, so he could do what he felt he had always wanted to do, to be a stay-at-home dad. Before I knew it, I was off to EARN the next biggest thing. We had established that I enjoy working and I would be okay being gone most of the time and he could be home with the kids. He was more patient and didn't mind doing house duties. It seemed like the perfect world that I could continue to control. But the problem was, I had already started having doubts and uncertainty about having kids at this point. I was in the middle of graduate school and I just started to worry that maybe I shouldn't be a mom. Maybe, I am not supposed to be a mom. Will I have time for my kids, will I be able to be there for them and love them how they needed to be loved? Will I be able to guide them and be present enough to make sure that they know that they are enough? Can I be the mother that they need? And sure enough, all it took was questions in my head to start triggering lies. I started hearing, "You won't be a good mom because you will be gone. You won't be able to pick up on how to love them because you will be distracted and exhausted. Plus, you don't want to find your body more repulsive and more disgusting since you can't even look fit before kids. It is probably not a good idea to be a mom." I heard Satan's whispers, and I was buying them.

What should the next stage in life look like for us?

It was a hot summer evening in Arlington, Texas that again, through lots of tears, failed tests, many, many prayers, and miraculous events, I received an advanced degree that I had fought hard for and felt I sacrificed much for. After graduation, I was determined to live life my way! I would start practicing as a nurse practitioner in an emergency room where I would be challenged and, once again, be able to perform, start paying off debt, travel, and enjoy the high life like never before.

For me, earning an advanced degree was the ultimate "sense of control" for a medical professional like me. I had opportunities to feel more secure, to feel better about my own efforts, to help change lives, to care for others, and to please others with my performance. I was constantly surrounded by smart people, by overachievers, by people who sacrifice a lot every day. I will never forget the sacrifices I watched being made every day. It kept me on my toes for sure and was an oh-so-familiar rodeo. I felt that if I continued in life working extra hard for everything I was involved in, much like all the other people I was around, it would keep this little void filled up and, just maybe, it would make God proud of me. And, just maybe, I would be proud of me.

I remember working in an isolated area of the emergency room in the middle of the night one night with alarms going off, everyone running around crazy, crying kids, frustrated parents, staff irritated with each other, (all doing a greater good), but just an overwhelming feeling of unexplainable darkness came over me. As I looked around, it was like everything stood still in a dark haze. After my shift, I drove home in the wee hours of the morning and this darkness continued as I woke up the next morning. I woke up alone. I had worked overnight, so my husband often left and I never realized it. But, before we knew it, this had become our life most weeks, and for the previous three years my husband and I had been working our own separate ways and I was alone. For the first time, I was exactly where I thought I was supposed to be, but I was so alone and in the dark.

I began feeling out of control, overwhelmed, not normal. My thoughts were dark and depressive, and I found myself not wanting to do life on a lot of days or I would just not feel much at all. When I did, it was an overwhelming feeling of, 'I have it all, I am supposed to be happy, but I am not. I am not happy, and I cannot find anything to be happy about.' These feelings became my reality. I started having unnecessary distrust in my husband, fear that I was unlovable, fear that I was making mistakes at the hospital, fear that I couldn't have meaningful friendships, and fear that life will never be great. Life felt like it was spinning out of control. I couldn't shake these thoughts.

My husband and I tried to connect through trips and through fun with friends. I tried to see my primary care physician seeking help for depression and was basically laughed at. My marriage seemed to be the priority and we needed help. We had been going our own way for so long, it was difficult. It seemed impossible.

But God is sovereign – God was with me. He knew how I felt and made himself available to me. God was in our marriage struggles and pointed us to a marriage mentor who allowed us to talk and made us feel normal and gave us hope. We were also around Godly friends who helped encourage us too, and helped us understand that all marriages struggle. We knew things wouldn't be perfect, but we also knew we couldn't just throw in the towel. I knew I needed to grow personally and find tools to fight off the negative feelings I was having all the time. God brought things like volunteering at our church in the special needs ministry into our lives and it helped make us feel connected to Christ and something bigger.

God is gracious- Although I was working all hours of the day and night, weekends, holidays, and was unbelievably tired, I was being introduced to so many amazing people. I was getting to watch some of the best medical providers and staff in the country serve and teach people like me. It was humbling, scary, and often super emotionally and spiritually dark. I had trouble wrapping my head around my feelings and the things I saw for years, but I knew God allowed me to be there for a reason. I knew I was serving a purpose and I am forever thankful for the experience.

God is the only way- Through this "highlight reel" time of being a new nurse practitioner, earning more money than we had ever had, being scared and seeing a different side of human life and illness, enjoying life as we could and still having a hard time connecting in my marriage, God was constant. He was still showing up to speak to me through sermons, through people I worked with, faithful friends, and through a new lifestyle coaching opportunity that I became involved in. God was showing me that He is what I needed, and He is the only way. Most days I was too busy to see this, but I knew he was there.

I continued to do "me," I kept working extra hard, I kept striving for excellence. I knew deep down, God had me where he needed me, but I wasn't sure for what reason and for why. During several of my un-preferred night shifts when I was exhausted and frustrated, I began to feel darkness again, an overwhelming sense of hopelessness in my own life, and I knew it was exactly what so many of my colleagues were feeling, too. I caught a glimpse of "why" and believed God needed me to experience some of this and feel the way I felt so that someday I could be a source of light, a vessel for His hope.

During my long, weary shift that night, I saw something. I saw beautiful diversity among my colleagues and I made a profound connection I had never made before. I saw other dark and hurting people in medicine for some specific reason. Some were ill as a child or had a life experience that gave them a desire to give back, make a difference, and earn a decent living. Others, like myself, who felt less than for so long, are drawn to medicine because it allows us to fill up voids in our hearts of not feeling good enough and not feeling like we matter. So, to prove to ourselves that we are smart, we are good enough, and we are appreciated, we serve others to help us feel good and this helps a lot of people numb different feelings of the past.

Until you are exhausted, until you are alone at home, until something happens on shift, until you start to believe lies or can't take the "shift work façade anymore"… then what? What will numb the disconnect, the discontentment, the pain?

What I learned for me, personally, in the wee hours of the morning, was a mixture of the two. I wanted to earn a living that would provide a comfortable lifestyle for my family, I wanted to impact other's lives and know that I made a difference, and I wanted to feel like I mattered.

But like with many other practitioners and providers, there are many days, due to different circumstances, that you are made to feel like you don't matter. That you are not enough, that you are not valued or appreciated.

What do you do to feel better again? Do you binge eat in front of the TV for hours to numb the pain? Do you consume large amounts of wine in the evenings to distract and help with sleeping? Do you look for something else to focus your energy on so that once again you feel better and feel like enough?

What do we do?

For the next three years of my nurse practitioner career, I refused to give up on what I thought was the best fit for me. I wanted to be great; I wanted to be proud and make others proud. In my head, I needed to feel in control, so I kept working hard, things were better, and for a short time, I felt like I was in control.

Until one day I was pregnant and yet again I was NOT in control.

Looking back, God tends to have a sense of humor like that, especially with us control freaks. I believe if you are in Jesus, you need to get used to wearing your seatbelt because when we are on His path, it's going to get bumpy and you're likely going to get thrown around a lot. He needs us to do things His way so that we experience the life He has for us, and you never know what that is going to look like.

I certainly didn't know what to think, feel, or do. And I am embarrassed to admit, I was not happy about this news.

I had recently lost weight that I had been trying to get off, I was at the height of my career, I was comfortable, we were leaving on an all-inclusive trip to Mexico soon, I was dealing with the darkness in the ER pretty well now, I finally felt in control of my life, and THIS was, well, out of my control. And y'all, I had almost resolved in my head that maybe I shouldn't be a mom.

So, I was scared. It took me a bit to reason all of my feelings, but it wasn't that I didn't want it, I was terrified.

Throughout the next nine months there were a lot of emotions. Mostly fear. Fear of gaining weight, fear of never being able to look at myself in the mirror without being disgusted, fear of not being there for my child because I was working all the time, fear of not being able to love him the way he needed to be loved, and fear that the distance between my husband and I would grow further. I was so scared, and this fear consumed me for the majority of my pregnancy. Much like the darkness I had experienced working in the ER that was unexplainable, I felt the fear like a weighted vest on me for many months. It took over, covering up the joy of pregnancy. I didn't know how to fight back so I didn't, I just kept going.

We had our precious firstborn on a beautiful evening in November and, thankfully, this allowed a few layers of scales to start falling off of my eyes. I was getting tiny glimpses of Jesus and His unconditional love for me. If I can love a baby this much, how much more does our Heavenly Father love me? Little did I know, my son was a gift, the vessel for the beginning of my redemption story, and the legacy of our family.

During the first few months after my son was born, the Lord started to reveal to me more about this darkness that I experienced. It was the schemes of Satan. It was the presence of the enemy that I had so plainly experienced. I thought that because I grew up in church that maybe I was excluded from warfare and intentional acts of Satan. I thought that if I begged hard enough, or prayed hard enough, or worked hard enough, then things would get better, much like when I failed my way through both of my undergraduate and graduate degrees. It all still worked out, so I assumed that "I" could make the darkness go away.

I didn't realize that Satan would use certain situations in which we are vulnerable emotionally and spiritually to attack and do everything he can to keep darkness around us, because he knows that where there is light, darkness cannot prevail. He knew what seeds he was planting even when I was in elementary. He knew the seeds he had planted about my body image, about not being good enough or worthy or valuable, about not being a good mom, about not being loving or lovable. Satan is very intentional with his attacks.

He knows that our purpose cannot be lived out when we believe His lies. So, he will come after you and me intentionally.

He kept coming around and for the next two years I was living under this disbelief that I needed to fight harder for control and that I must be a failure because no matter what I did, I continued to be out of control, to feel less than, to feel not good enough. I was completely and overly exhausted as by this time we had added to our family. Now I had two kids in less than two years and I continued to work days, nights, and weekends, and my husband continued to be a stay-at-home dad. I remember so vividly when the once profound thoughts (fears, insecurities, depression) that I was having about my body, my marriage, my role as a mother, my career, roles as a friend, coach, and mentor, started to become my reality. No matter what others told me or thought of me, I was not capable, I was not good at what I was doing, I couldn't be enough.

No matter what others thought I looked like, I was fat and disgusting and refused to look at myself in the mirror most days. I was lazy when I couldn't get up early to work out because I was exhausted from work and taking care of a newborn, I was unlovable, I was a bad mom, I was unworthy, I was never going to be enough or make God proud.

I had been speaking so negatively to myself and had resolved that there was no hope for a normal life or to ever feel in control again and I knew that I needed Jesus. In a real, raw, simple, and reviving way.

You see, I grew up in church and I knew Jesus, most Bible stories, and most popular verses. I knew He had shown up for me on many occasions when I would beg and plead. But

I did not KNOW Jesus. I did not know his unending, unconditional, unwavering love. The kind of love that says, there is NOTHING that you can do, have done, will do, should do that can make me love you more or that can separate you from me. He loves me and you so much. PERIOD.

I knew I needed this kind of love and I finally wanted to understand it.

I needed to start hearing from Jesus in an intimate way every day. Trust me, I fought it and thought there was no way this busy working medical momma has "extra" time to spend with Jesus. But I knew something needed to change. And you know what they say, "If you want things to change in your life, you have to change some things you are doing in your life." So, I started searching for something simple. I had attempted many Bible studies and could never complete them or just felt overwhelmed every time. And at this point, I didn't need to feel "more Christian" by doing a lengthy study or being involved in a profound Bible study. I just needed Jesus, simply His word and prayer. So, I searched and searched and started finding Scripture reading and writing calendars.

My type A personality loves a calendar, so this is where my redemption story began.

Every day, I started following this simple plan. I found and followed other peoples' plans, then I created my own plan.

It was through this time of simple Scripture and Truth that he told me to leave my nurse practitioner career. Beyond the struggle of work-life balance, God wanted to use me elsewhere. Yes, in my heart, I had known he was calling me to something different, something more, something beyond me.

I was very reluctant to even believe this request was from the Lord. Maybe I was just so exhausted and becoming desperate to change my situation, but leaving altogether? Not possible. Medicine is ME, it's who I am. My family depended on me for our livelihood, our insurance, and our security as my husband was at home.

I heard God's request, but tried to pretend like it didn't happen and I kept going on with life.

After two years of disobedience I was miserable. Anxiety was at its all-time high with constant feelings of uncertainty. Waves of depression came from feelings of isolation and shame for wanting to leave healthcare, guilt of putting my family at risk for leaving, feelings of inadequacy, and feeling like I was completely crazy for even thinking that God would use someone like me to encourage and motivate others through Him.

I began to feel so dark again. I began to live as unworthy, not capable, not good enough, unlovable, never qualified. I was going through the motions of Scripture but not believing it.

I felt there was nothing that I could do to earn His favor. At times I was angry and bitter.

On one of my darkest days, I had an experience, literally felt captured and imprisoned by the enemy and it's something I will never forget. I was trying to send messages to some amazing ladies to encourage them and invite them to join one of my online challenge groups because this was one of the few things that was keeping me sane and because I needed to be positive for them. I was in my car before an evening clinic shift trying to get my composure to send the messages and I just couldn't shake a feeling of suffocation. Like the devil himself had his hands around my mouth and neck, pushing me down, and I was hearing the ole so familiar tunes… You are not worthy, you are not capable, you are not smart enough to do your job, you will never have a great marriage, your boys will remember that you were gone a lot and feel disconnected from you, you will never be able to make a difference… you are not who you think you are.

I was sweating and crying, and I remember thinking I was completely nuts. I was convinced that I needed to check myself into a mental health facility. I needed help. I was able to call a mentor and I quickly sent a text to a few friends asking for prayer. I had heard another mentor say when she first wakes up in the morning, she starts her day with "Thank you Jesus, thank you Jesus, thank you Jesus," because His name casts out the devil himself. So, to protect her mind she proclaims Him first thing. Well, I began to say, "Thank you JESUS, thank you Jesus." And the weight was slowly lifted.

I was torn, scared, beyond confused, and just desperate for God to change my circumstance. "I" was doing everything in my power to change my circumstances and nothing was changing. What more can I do?

I had been praying for a breakthrough with my lifestyle coaching business. Through my intentional prayer time each morning, the Lord had recently revealed to me that He needed me to host Women's events. To minister to them, love them, and share His truth with them. I was even more confused. "Why, God, aren't you changing things? God… hurry up already. I am ready."

But I realized in that attack, that I continued to believe these lies of Satan, these schemes of attack. Not only was I hearing Satan tell lies to me, I was now saying negative things about myself every day and I was believing them.

I realized that all these years, those little seeds that Satan had intentionally planted as far back as elementary had been growing and I felt were part of me. They grew and grew and before I knew It, I was constantly telling lies to myself and believing them. Every day this had become my life.

I needed a tool to fight back. I needed to change the way I was speaking to myself.

I started listening to sermons, podcasts, reading books, and declaring Gods truth in my life every day.

I started learning declarations of truth or positive affirmations. I certainly needed this so much. I needed to change the way I was speaking to myself.

Even if I didn't feel it, I needed to declare truth. Because I knew that what I speak about, I bring about.

When I felt insecure, I would declare, "I am strong, I am capable."

When I started avoiding myself in the mirror and speaking negatively, I would declare, "I am in the best shape of my life. Thank you, Jesus, that I am at my ideal weight."

When I felt unlovable, I would say things like, "I am worthy. I am highly favored."

So, I started adding an affirmation or declaration of truth to my Scripture calendar.

It was helping reshape my mind and my heart, it was profound, and this was where I needed to be to allow the Lord to start revealing Himself to me. I needed to be still to know what God was trying to do. (Psalm 46:10)

God began to show me many things personally during my morning routine, but my marriage continued to have a wedge and be a struggle. I knew work had to be done here.

Our marriages are gifts and must be a priority, but we found ourselves in a place of desperation, a fork in the road. I was working and gone a lot, exhausted when home, and felt unlovable. He was a stay-at-home dad, cooking, cleaning, taking care of the kids, and felt unappreciated, unloved, at times insecure and unprovider-like. At this point, he had already been applying for jobs to take some weight off of me and get out of the house, but God was slamming doors left and right.

He was disappointed and quite honestly, I didn't want him away, but I was hurt that he was hurt. But, I was in control and that's how I liked it. We were a complete mess.

It was during this time of desperation in both of our lives that God orchestrated a divine appointment with a counselor almost an hour away from our home. We had never been to counseling, but knew this might be our only option. The counselor typically only ministered to families who were in the ministry but took a special consideration and basically did a friend a favor to see us. And he could only meet at 12 o'clock noon on a Tuesday. What? Who can do that?

We could! I happened to be off most Tuesdays, the kids were in preschool, and my husband didn't work. So, when I say that God was up to something, he was up to something.

Through this dark time and our eight months of counseling, the Lord brought water into a drought that had been going on for years. We even started to see green grass right where we were as it was being watered. God was made real to us through this experience and His unconditional love was brought before us in an unforgettable way.

God is sovereign- God truly provided an angel to guide us in our dry marriage. Our relationship was a complete mess and we needed help. Our counselor allowed the Lord to work through him and it was life-changing. We know that the things that we were shown and what we experienced was divine. God showed me scars and wounds that I didn't even realize I had. He showed my husband things he was carrying around. He revealed wedges in our lives individually and things that were turning into walls between us and counseling allowed us to start breaking down these walls and rebuild the connection between us the right way, God's way.

God is gracious- While going to counseling and changing the way I was speaking to myself, expecting God to show us His plan, things were changing. During an intentional time of prayer over the course of a few days, God opened up a perfect job opportunity for my husband. This job is something that has allowed him to thrive, learn, grow, and have Godly mentorship and guidance on many levels. I knew I had to give up control and when I did, God graciously provided His perfect solution. It was also during this time that God made very clear to me His purpose and His plan for me, which is to continue ministering to women, but in ways that only He can provide, like motivational speaking, writing, and for our family to host women's and marriage events long-term on a ranch that He would provide.

<u>God is the only way-</u> We were desperate, but we were willing. And when you are willing, HE is going to show you THE way. Most often, God has so many things planned for us, but we are so selfish and doubt too much that we won't even take the first steps towards him, so we can see the hope we all so desperately need. This was me and this was us. Even if we proclaim that HE is the way, the truth, the life, if we are not willing to walk towards him and let him guide us, nothing changes. I thank God every day we said "yes" to change, to help, to do things Gods way.

As this season continued, nearly a year had gone by after God revealed himself to me in such a real and new way. I began to see my redemption. His love for me that has covered it all prevents me from having to strive and work for His favor. And this is such a beautiful thing. Through counseling and the intentional time, I was spending with Him every day, I finally understood God's unconditional love for me and that my efforts should be out of grateful obedience and no longer out of earning favor.

I remember starting to feel more peaceful on more days than I had ever felt. I knew some way, somehow, a breakthrough was coming, and my doubt was getting less and less. There was NO clear 'how' and 'what' to do, but I just knew things were going to change. I was still practicing in healthcare and still growing daily with the Lord. Some days, my old selfish ways slip back in, Satan triggers a negative thought, or something happens and I can quickly slap on the negative Nancy cap.

But I knew God was not finished writing my story, just like he wasn't finished with my marriage. I had profound hope in Him.

I continued to LEAN IN to the Lord, seek Him, read and write His word, kept it simple, affirmed His Truth in my life every day, and God started to put puzzle pieces together for me. He started helping me make sense of my mess. And better yet, he started to show me His miracles in all of the mess.

I told the Lord that I knew he was up to something, but I wanted Him to show me my next steps. I had wanted to get help in my business so that I could have better balance with working two jobs and a home life. So, I reached out for help.

I will never forget this meeting on a hot summer day in a coffee shop before I went in for an evening shift. I had put word out that I needed help with some graphic and marketing duties for my coaching business and was meeting a candidate. Her humble professionalism, honest joy, and divine presence were undeniable. I was overwhelmed and grateful to get to partner with such a gem. She would be an awesome asset and new friend.

I shared my story of where I had come from, where I was, and where I was headed, and we both had tears in our eyes. She proceeded to share that she was glad to help me with my business the best she could, but she felt strongly that we were introduced so that I could meet her father, who had a similar story of leaving a cooperate career to pursue what God had called him to do. He is now a motivational speaker, a writer, and owns a publishing company. She felt certain she was to be the vessel for our meeting. Our business relationship started, and God was working behind the scenes.

Things were going great.

Just a few short months later, we got word that the clinic where I worked was being bought out and lots of changes were about to happen. There could be a few options for me, but the only one I saw was that this was Gods way of telling me, "NOW IS THE TIME. I am opening this door for you, you don't even have to kick it down, and it's time you walk through and plan to meet me on the other side." I was extremely confident in this request by this point, but my husband's doubt made several weeks very difficult. This step would be a dramatic decrease in earnings and there were no clear next steps regarding speaking, writing, or my coaching career. I didn't know what God had planned, but GOD plainly told me, "NOW IS THE TIME, and until you jump, you'll never see how I will make you soar and take care of you." He said, "You've done enough. I promise I will take care of you and I will do more than you can possibly imagine, if you will just practice what you preach, BELIEVE, and have true FAITH."

So, I put in my two-week notice, leaving healthcare after 14 years. The day I left my last shift, I have never had more confidence in the Lord and in His provision and plan because for the first time ever, I WAS NOT IN CONTROL. There was nothing more I could do to earn His favor. His death and resurrection, my redemption, and His sovereign provision in my life, all the things that He had been revealing to me, were my forever FREEDOM. For the first time I was being truly obedient and I felt free.

After I left, the Lord allowed me a few weeks to rest and reflect on His goodness before Satan tried to create panic and doubt. I believe he wanted me to experience life without striving, to just be obedient and experience what working for the Lord looked like instead of working for my own glory.

He showed me that my identity was in Him, not my work, not the income I was bringing in, but that I am valuable and valued despite anything I could ever do. I am precious and worthy no matter what.

I am the Daughter of the Most High King. That's who I am.

That's who you are!

The ways of the Lord are good. When we fully surrender, he will literally guide us to and hand us our next steps.

God is sovereign- Within a month of leaving my career as a nurse practitioner, the Lord asked me to bring my Scripture reading and writing calendar to life in a book. I had been praying and asking God how to get this much-needed tool into the hands of so many other overwhelmed, tired, and weary mommas' hands. He saw my heart, my daily discipline in seeking and affirming His truth daily, and I had favor. My business assistant introduced me to her father who had become my mentor and also owned a publishing company. So, the Lord literally brought me opportunity. He literally allowed everything to fall into place in record time to publish my first book within 6 weeks and in less than 3 months from leaving my medicine career. My calendar was brought to life into a #1 best-selling book and His sovereign hand was involved in so much of the detail. In preparing for this, he was literally putting things in my life along the way that were undeniably HIS way.

God is gracious- His grace continues to cover me, my new career, my marriage, my parenting, my ministry, my relationships, my coaching team, and my clients. God placed me here on this earth to love my family and be the light in my home first, and then to motivate and encourage you through His grace and love. Like John 13:14-17 says, 'So If I, the master and the teacher, washed your feet, you must now wash other's feet… If you understand what I am telling you, act like it—go bless others and live a blessed life.'

God was so patient and so loving, watching me strive and do my own thing for so long, but He embraced me and washed my feet, washed me of all my guilt and shame and insecurities and inadequacies. I got it. I get it and my heart is so profoundly passionate about extending this love and grace and to wash your feet, to be his light, a voice, the vessel that empowers you, grooms you, and shows you His Truth in love. (Ephesians 4:15)

<u>God is life</u>- He is life. We can only find true life in Him. Without Him, we are in darkness. For so many years, I had a little flicker of light that he lit so many years ago when I said "yes" to Jesus. That light was always there, His presence was always there. But you see, I covered it up with so much, with my effort, with my insecurities, with my attempt to do more, be more, feel better. Although on the outside I accomplished much, and it might have seemed perfect, my addiction to self-sufficiency proved to be detrimental to my mental and physical health, my relationships, my career, my entire world. Without Him, I can live, just like you can live, but there is no true freedom, no true life.

Dear Striving Soul,

I hear you, my soul connects with you, my life has been you.

We have been sought out by Satan to be tied down with the bondage of hurt, shame, pain, insecurities, feelings of worthlessness, and to feel so lost and defeated that we feel we are too far from His love, grace, and hope. But Christ is standing behind the rejection and negative voices we hear, with his arms open wide, waiting to enfold us in the security of His truth.

The Truth is that you are precious, you are accepted, you are enough.

No matter what choices you have made and often make, His love is not based on performance.

Christ's love for you is based on His perfect surrender on the cross.

You have to choose to accept this LOVE, His love, and walk in this truth for it to make a difference in how you journey through life.

You have to choose Jesus, His love, His way.

And then our striving can cease, because in Christ, we are free!

Motivating and encouraging you through His love and grace,

Cheneil
(The Momma Motivator)

About the Author – Cheneil Torbert

Cheneil, a faith-based, full-time professional motivator, a lifestyle coach, mentor, and a speaker. She also holds her certification as an Acute Care Pediatric Nurse Practitioner. She resides in Texas with her husband of 13 years and two preschool boys. She is an outgoing, energetic, daughter of the King who loves health, wellness, coffee and Jesus. She is passionate about helping women, like you understand God's truth, His unconditional, unwavering love for you, and helping you see it and live in it out in the midst of your everyday messy life.

Cheneil's heart is for YOU, encouraging you, and motivating you through your mess. Because it's through this mess that God is making Miracles. She shares her heart and passion with you in many ways:

• Monthly Interactive Faith Calendar: online community of women who need a plan, encouragement, and accountability.

• Individualized Faith-Based Online Lifestyle Coaching to help you on a more personal level with your health and wellness.

• Motivational Faith-Based Speaking on Lifestyle & Healthy Living for your next Women's event.

She loves Motivating you through His Grace & Love

Get to know her by following The Momma Motivator on Facebook! It's your source for motivational videos, daily truth and encouragement!

Cheneil Torbert
Professional Motivator, Lifestyle Coach &
Nurse Practitioner
Learn more about her services and contact her at:
www.cheneiltorbert.com
903-235-4203

Chapter 4 – A Striving Soul Finds Freedom

Chapter 5

I Hear You
By Kelly Castor

As I was walking across the courtyard, I heard my voice. I saw who I was talking to, but I found myself feeling like a third party, an innocent bystander listening in on someone else's conversation. I was talking to the owner of the company I worked for. I was letting him know, point by point, how he hadn't lived up to his end of the bargain. What he hadn't fulfilled. What he had promised and either not provided or had taken away. It was all so familiar. And then it hit me. It *was* familiar. It's what I had said to several of my past employers. The fact is, I'd heard the story before.

I then started searching for the commonalities. I heard a voice in my head emphatically say, "What's the common denominator?" Was it the same industry? *No.* Same type of position? *No.* It was a completely new type of position for me. Was it the same situation? *No!* Once again, it was an entirely new situation. In fact, it wasn't even the same state! I had just moved to Texas from Indiana, so it couldn't be a geographic or cultural thing. And then it dawned on me. The common denominator was "me." Let me say this again, "I" was the common denominator. It wasn't my boss, my company, my circumstances, or my environment. It was *me*.

This wasn't the first time that I'd come to the realization that I needed to look in the mirror. But this time was one of the most meaningful and life-changing events in my life. I was 25.

I've had other, "look in the mirror moments" before *and* since, but I can look back at this time and honestly say this was one of those key moments in time that literally changed the trajectory of my life. The simple, yet powerful understanding that "I" was the common denominator.

So you might be thinking, "I get it. It's about taking responsibility and being accountable for your own actions." That's true, but it's just the tip of the iceberg of the impact and depth of this one simple realization.

"Being" is more important than "Doing"

Ralph Waldo Emerson wrote, "Who you are speaks so loudly I can't hear what you're saying." I've found that we humans spend an inordinate amount of time perplexed, trying to figure out how or why our words and actions aren't getting through to others and why we aren't getting the results we were expecting or wanting.

As a Leadership Development consultant, I deal with some version of this seemingly every day. The most classic is, "I've asked them if there's anything wrong or if they are having any trouble and they keep saying everything is fine." This usually comes on the heels of this "leader" telling me with pride how, "Everyone knows who I am. I tell it like it is. I don't pull any punches." Think about that for a moment. The leader is saying, "Who I am is strong, straight-forward, no holds barred." But... "I want people to be vulnerable with me. I want them to challenge my assumptions. I want them to be honest if they disagree." Do you see any conflicts here? Who they are "being" is speaking so loudly that no one can actually hear or believe that it's "ok" to disagree, to open up, to be vulnerable.

Another term for this is presence. Our presence, who we are "being," is what gives our words and actions power and influence. If you want to be a leader, whether in business or at church, at the Boy Scouts or even in your own family, your presence is dictating your ability to be effective every bit as much as your words and actions.

Here's an example in business, but do your best to translate it to your own personal life as well. Rather than focus on your "to-do" list exclusively, create another short list first. I call this the "to-be" list. Here's how I suggest you do this. In the morning, write down who you want to "be" in 3 words. An example is: Today I want to be "patient, a good listener, a motivator." Throughout the day you will be amazed as you move from one situation to another, how this will pop up for you and you will start the process of being conscious of who you are 'being' as much as what you are 'doing.' When done consistently, your impact and contribution expand dramatically, allowing you to be a more positive light for everyone you encounter.

As a side note to this, in business I suggest a daily practice. Write down 3 "to-be's," 3 "to-do's," and at the end of the day write down 3 "Learnings." I know most of us have many more to-do's than three, but it's important to be clear what 3 actions move the needle the most towards our goals. By doing this daily, you start to make significant strides on things most important to you rather than just being able to 'check the box' on 12 items without understanding how they really impact you in terms of achieving your most important goals.

The "3 Learnings" round out the day, helping us reflect in a way that is about going forward. What did I learn today that is impactful for tomorrow? Some days I can put the pen to paper and immediately write three or four or five things that I learned that day, no problem. Other days I find myself struggling to find one thing worth writing. Just like physical workouts, the raw power of this is the daily exercise – of taking a few moments to reflect and look for the lessons that are available to all of us throughout each and every day.

Examples of some "Learnings" may be noticing the impact of my awareness in who I was 'being' throughout the day. Other times, it's about where I got so focused on the action that I was unaware of the cost of accomplishing it in terms of the relationships of those around me.

This is especially true in family relationships. It's always puzzling to me why we treat those closest to us the worst. In fact, I once asked a friend of mine, August Turak, who wrote a great book entitled *Business Secrets of the Trappist Monks*, about this phenomenon of treating those closest to us the worst and he simply answered, "Because we can." I felt this was profound and also sad. We owe it to ourselves to be conscious of who we are "being" to those around us, especially our closest loved ones.

Focusing on who we are being, taking action on things that have the most impact towards our goals, and pausing to learn a few simple things each and every day can have a tremendous impact on preventing us from treating those closest to us the worst. In fact, I believe it raises the bar on all of our relationships. It puts us in a position to have a positive impact on those around us, our tasks at hand, and also our own goals and dreams. In essence, it's key to being a true leader.

So, the next time you are getting ready to go into a meeting of any kind, pause and ask yourself, "Who do I want to be in this meeting that best serves everyone involved?" Then you will start to develop a slightly different version of Emerson's great quote - "Who you are being speaks so loudly that I hear what you are saying in a way that is more influential and meaningful to me."

Give it a try – The 3 To-Be's, 3 To-Do's and the 3 Learnings – every day.

"Do What you say, When you say."

After he answered the phone and I said 'hello' he said, "Wow, I'll say this for you. When you say you'll call, you do it every time and right on time." I, frankly, don't recall anything else that was said on that call. I was a little amazed at how something so simple had made such a strong impression on him. It was just the way I was brought up. I was 19.

My father instilled in me that your word was your bond. He never said those words to me or anything like that. He just lived it. When he said he was going to do something by a certain time or show up somewhere at a certain time, he did it. He didn't "try" to do it. He did it. As I moved on in life I had other instances where people remarked to me that I was on time or followed through as if it was something unique. The older I got and the more I moved up in the corporate world, I saw time and time again why they were so shocked. My personal opinion is there is an epidemic flowing through our society that is one of not viewing our words as commitment. Trust me when I tell you this: We are all human, especially me. I'm certain someone will read this and remember when I didn't do something that I said I was going to do. But I also know this, it won't be close to the number of times or the number of people who would remark that I do what I say, when I say, not because I'm something special, but because I pay attention to it. I work at it. It's important to me as a leader, but more importantly as a human being.

I've taken a poll at many events where I was speaking or leading a training to prove my point. Here's how I do it. I urge you to participate as you read this.

How many people do you have in your life that absolutely, 100% of the time, do what they say every time, without fail, to the point that if they don't, your first thought is not of frustration, but of concern? You'd actually be worried. You might even say something like, "Wow. This isn't like Maggie at all. I hope she's ok. I'm certain something serious must have come up." I ask them to show a number of fingers on one or both hands to indicate how many people fit these criteria in their own lives. How many did you come up with? Most of the time people rarely get past one hand. Sometimes it might be six or seven, but I'm telling you that's a rare occasion and I've done this multiple times in small work teams and in large halls with a ton of people.

You might think that's enough to prove my point but we've only covered half of the equation. Now I ask you, how many people of the four or five that you already identified not only do what they say, but they do it *when they say*? This is another layer that once again cuts the number. At this point, we typically only have two or three people left that we absolutely can count on doing what they say, *when they say*. I don't know what you ended up with, but what's really important is to understand the power of being one of those few to those around you. My belief is that if you do what you say, when you say, you are in the top 1 or 2% in both business and life.

Think about that. If you do what most of us would consider to be a common courtesy, consistently, you will be considered in the upper percentile to those around you. This means you may get opportunities that others won't. You'll be able to help others that you wouldn't have had the chance to otherwise. You'll have the opportunity to be a "leader" among those you interact with, not necessarily because of your title, but because you become worthy of someone's time and attention.

As a leader, this is invaluable. If you are someone that your people believe you will do what you say, when you say, not only have you raised the bar on their own personal expectations, but you've developed the key ingredient of trust. Trust is a foundational element of any relationship.

As a leader you must work on developing what I call a "Leadership Relationship" with your people. Having them trust you and see you as someone who can help them grow to the next level is critical if you are going to lead a high-performance team of any kind.

Start simply in building this type of relationship with those around you by "Doing what you say, when you say." By doing this, you will stand above the crowd, which will inspire you to be a better leader in both words and actions.

Take 100% Ownership

I had been the Sales Manager for about two weeks. It was the first time I'd been a sales manager and I had inherited two salespeople in a new office that I was to grow to six to eight people. One of them was a young, highly-motivated, and competent guy. He was on a mission to be more and do more. At a later date, he told me he took this position because he needed direct sales experience so that he could start his own business. He was driven, smart, and clear. He was also "green" in sales. But make no mistake, he was a keeper and I was intent on making sure he grew as a salesperson. I was 27.

I got a call from my boss that we had a new customer, sold by this driven young guy, but the conversion had not gone smoothly and they were threatening to cancel. I met with my rep and said, "Let's go see them." My rep could brief me on the details on the way over.

My rep was clearly upset on a couple of fronts. First, this was a big sale for him that he'd worked very hard on in a competitive situation and he did not want to lose it, especially because of something that was "completely out of his control." Second, he felt he was personally at risk of "losing face" with the client. In other words, his reputation was at risk. As we were getting off of the elevator walking into their office, I told him not to worry, I'd handle it. I had no idea what I was going to do.

As I introduced myself and extended my hand to the owner of the client company I said, "I'm here to take care of your situation in a way that is good for you. Whatever that is, I'm here to make that happen." He acknowledged that and then we got into the conversation very quickly. As I listened to him and gained a clear understanding of where he was and what his perspective was, something came over me that made it clear what the next step was.

When he finished I asked a few questions to clarify some points and then said, "First off, I want you to know that I personally own this situation. My representative did everything right. You put your trust and faith in him and our company and we owe both of you an apology. But more importantly, I own resolving this for you."

I won't bore you with the details of what happened next, but as we were leaving, the owner of the client company stuck out his hand and said some version of, "Thank you for owning this issue and not pointing fingers at others involved. I'm looking forward to working with you and your company." To be clear, there were several entities involved in making this customer conversion happen: their previous provider, two third-party technical providers, and our own company. We were not responsible for the issue that happened. We did everything the way we're supposed to. Someone else dropped the ball. I didn't admit guilt. I admitted ownership.

As the elevator doors closed, my young salesman burst into a huge smile and jumped in the air and gave me a big high five! He said, "That was AWESOME! Thank you so much." Later that day I got a call from my boss who said that my rep had called him and said how happy he was that I was there as his manager. My boss (whom I'd known and worked with for many years) said he told him that he'd just gotten indoctrinated into the "Kelly Castor way of doing things."

To be clear here, this story isn't about me. It's about taking 100% ownership. It probably sounds simple when you read this. You might even be saying, "Well of course you should take responsibility. That's customer service 101!" And you'd be right. But it goes a little deeper than that.

There's a difference between responsibility and ownership. Responsibility is being the culprit or the one "holding the bag." Ownership is being the solution. This is subtle and powerful. It also is more of a way of "being" than a tactic. This ties in with "presence," as I mentioned earlier.

To apply this concept of taking 100% ownership, it doesn't have to be some lightning rod event like I just described. It's extremely useful in everything, from something as tactical as project management to something as invaluable as parenting. 100% ownership doesn't imply right or wrong. It implies commitment.

3 Powerful Truths

What I've just described is what I call "3 Powerful Truths."

Be who you want others to Be
Do what you say, When you say
Take 100% Ownership

I've utilized this thinking for many, many years and I've helped others adopt it personally and inject it into a corporate culture. It's a foundational piece to not only my business, but more importantly, to my life.

But as with most things in life, it's not so much what we know, whether it be a system, communication style, or any type of life tool, but it's how we employ what we know in a natural way.

The Still, Small Voice

Many people think the 3 Powerful truths are a "nice little saying and system." But it's actually foundationally built upon a much deeper level – listening to the little voice within. I believe it's the Holy Spirit. If you go back to the common denominator – the voice saying, "What is the common denominator?" That wasn't me being pragmatic, practical, brilliant or wise. It was the Holy Spirit breaking through the chatter in my own head so that I could be a conduit for God's will.

The underlying story here is less about tactics and systems and more about listening. It's about listening for the Holy Spirit. It's about spending time in those moments of quiet and experiencing the Holy Spirit.

We all have that voice in our heads that tells us what we did was right and wrong. The voice of judgment is what we tend to listen to the most and the one that speaks the loudest. "You suck! Why did you do that again? You always screw this up. Loser!" The voice of judgment is usually a bully, a liar, a naysayer. He or she is always the loudest. I know. When it comes to the voice of judgment, I have twins.

But if you think about the stories I spoke of, it wasn't the voice of judgment that I heard. It was the voice of wisdom. Compassion. The voice of love. The voice of God, the Holy Spirit. He's not a bully. He's not a liar. The Holy Spirit sometimes speaks up loud enough to drown out the voice of judgment, but it's never intimidating. God is always caring. He has your best interest in mind. The Holy Spirit is a gentle guide.

But He also gives us freedom of choice. We don't have to listen. We don't have to heed the advice. The Holy Spirit never says, "Well, you didn't listen to me so I'm just going to leave." God is committed. God is loyal. God is consistent.

What's not consistent is our ability to hear the still, small voice first, heed it second. The world is so full of noise and false flags in terms of what really matters. It's not about our possessions. It's not about our affluence. It's not about fame.

It's about human beings. It's about how we help others small and large. It can range from a smile and a thank you, to holding a loved one who is in distress and pain. It's helping those less fortunate. It's utilizing our talents and means to help others.

In full disclosure, I like having nice things. I like being able to give my loved ones nice things, things of convenience, beyond necessity. I'm not saying there's anything wrong with that. I'm just saying that's not what it's all about. But that's the noise of the world.

So how do we tap into the still small voice, the Holy Spirit that serves us in a way that serves others? I don't have the foolproof methods for this. I can only offer what has worked for me, albeit in an imperfect way. I'm human and I still work hard at listening for and to the small, still voice.

My first suggestion is to actually listen for the Holy Spirit. You might think of it in terms of a hunch or intuition. The first key is to recognize it. To be able to separate it from the chatter, the noise. This requires you to catch yourself dismissing a thought as not important. Have you ever had something come to mind that you paid no attention to, but then later when something happened you think, "I knew I should've done that." Or perhaps, "I thought of that." These are examples of us dismissing the wisdom of the Holy Spirit.

Think about it as if you were building or deepening a personal relationship with someone. You would spend time getting to know them. You would learn their voice inflections and their facial expressions. In building a strong relationship there is no substitute for time spent with them. If you take each of the examples I highlighted in my life, it included the still, small voice that prompted me in those situations. The still, small voice of the Holy Spirit. In the Bible, Jesus says "And I will pray the Father, and he will give you another Counselor, to be with you forever." (John 14:16) This is the Holy Spirit – the still, small voice.

As a trigger, I want you to catch yourself at least three times today, not tomorrow, but today, dismissing what seems like a passing thought. Examine the thought. What if you listened to and recognized it as the voice of God, the Holy Spirit? What would happen? Play it out and if it moves you towards something in a position of love or caring or compassion – if you know it is the right thing to do – do it. Listen to it.

Another suggestion is to ask for the presence to be aware of the voice of God. Here's how I do this. As a Leadership Development Consultant, I have many, many one-on-one sessions throughout the week. Before I start these, I take two to three minutes and say some version of this prayer.

Thank you, Lord, for the opportunity to do this work and be a conduit for Your will. Please help me quiet the chatter in my head so that I may hear Your words and feel Your will, so that as we work on solving these business issues, we are working on something much bigger, much more important. Please help us be open so that we can be filled with the Holy Spirit to the point that everyone we meet, everyone we think of, and everyone that thinks of us, is filled with that same Light. Please help us be conduits of your love, light, and will. All power and glory goes to You. Amen.

I utilize some version of this prayer before important meetings and conversations, before I start a training, or before I go on stage. I say it before I start writing or creating a program. It is my form of True North. It's my compass. I utilize it to tap into my true calling and also to help prevent me from getting too full of myself. Every time I start listening to myself for guidance, it never turns out like it does when I'm able to listen to the small, still voice, the Holy Spirit. When this happens, I feel like I'm tapped into my true self, my true purpose.

With this, I invite you to listen for, and to, the small, still voice - the voice of God.

About the Author – Kelly Castor

Kelly's life's work is centered around personal development for the greater good – the greater good in a department, organization, industry and life. Through his 30 years of leading and developing high-performance teams and organizations, he has developed a model of success that is replicable for any organization that is serious about being a leader in their respective field. Kelly started Velocity Leadership in 2002 with a clear mission - building high-performance organizations that serve all entities – company, customer and employee - in a way that is sustainable and creates a unique competitive advantage.

Kelly Castor is a Certified Marshall Goldsmith Stakeholder Centered Executive Coach and a High-Performance Organizational Consultant. He's available for keynotes, workshops and executive coaching. He speaks on the topics of Leadership, Developing High-Performance Cultures and Organizational Velocity – Speed *plus* Direction *minus* Drag. These three areas feed the common need in business: How to get a group of people moving in the same direction with a lot of velocity!

Prior to Velocity Leadership, in partnership with two other former telecom executives, Kelly launched NII Communications, a telecom company based in San Antonio, TX. NII Communications was subsequently sold to ClearTel Communications.

Kelly Castor is a firm believer in the human spirit and our capacity to achieve. He's spent the better part of his adult life observing and studying what it takes to engage and motivate individuals to the point of high performance. This is his passion.

To turn his passion into your results, Kelly can be reached at www.velldr.com

Chapter 5 – I Hear You

Chapter 6

My Heart Set Free – No Chains on Me!
By Judy Denney

As I sit here quietly in my home, a place that I call my **SAFE HAVEN** which God has so graciously provide for me, I never imagined that I would be here writing about my life's journey. It is a place where I find peace, solace, safety, hope, and faith. I find myself always reciting the Scripture in the stillness of night, "BE STILL AND KNOW THAT I AM GOD!" (Psalm 46:10). These words have kept me grounded and helped me to stay focused and continue to believe that God is still in the business of creating miracles.

My life has been like the many curves in the road, many times never knowing which direction to go. These curves were always accompanied with the fear of the unknown, judgment, rejection, and being condemned. My self-esteem and confidence were at its lowest level ever. My body felt like an empty shell and numb beyond words. Many times, I felt like I wasn't even in my own body, afraid and ashamed to look in the mirror at myself because of the way I looked. This beautiful vessel that God gave me was deteriorating right in front of my own eyes. I was too weak, fragile, and never had the strength to take care of it. I truly didn't know this person anymore and couldn't believe that my zest for life was gone.

However, during the curves in the road, one thing I learned is that no matter how well thought out my plans were, I would experience disappointments and joy. These would move me more deeply and help me grow in my personal and professional life. I discovered that the experience that I had to endure would be my roadmap to a new beginning and no matter when life throws a curve at me, I would embrace and learn from it.

I would try and reflect back to the beautiful person that I once knew. This girl always had a big smile, eyes sparkling, heart on fire with so much love, energy, faith, and hope. The life of the party one might say. Family, friends, and people from all walks of life would always compliment the compassion I had for people and life. It didn't matter to me about culture, race, or creed; we were all God's children and precious in his sight. I loved them unconditionally, the same way God loves me. I was always told that I had an aura about me that attracted people and made them feel loved, important, and cared for. Despite the storms that I was going through, in some small way God gave me the strength to take care of everyone and never say, 'no.' I was always available for family, friends, and strangers to listen to, console, and direct them in the right path, no matter what barriers they were struggling with. I was always going above and beyond the call of duty and wanting to ensure that it was like "no child left behind." However, I was the child that was left behind because my own commitments to provide support and a shoulder for others to lean on did not allow myself the time to focus on my well–being.

This strong, brave, independent, career-driven, outgoing girl was living in a dark and hopeless world. I was very active in the church, from teaching Sunday school and children's church to singing in the church choir, playing the bass drum, and singing duets. I was now too weak, embarrassed, and fragile to reach out for help. I was afraid of exposing the other side of this dark and hopeless world that I was living in. A world that so many of my family and friends thought was made in heaven and could only dream of. I was living in a fake world and suppressing all my pain, hurts, disappointments, scares, and protecting everyone that I loved.

However, with my ongoing faith in God, family and friends, I saw a ray of hope. I started my life's journey at a very young age. Like any young girl, I dreamt about a life that would consist of being happily married with children and grandchildren, looking forward to the golden years and growing old gracefully. I married at the tender age of 18 and soon became a mother. It was a life-changing experience in many ways. God blessed me with a beautiful son who stole my heart the moment I held him in my arms. His big blue eyes, chubby cheeks, and dark hair lit up the hospital room. I held his soft, gentle hand in mine and touched his soft body; it was a connection like none other. God gave me a gift that I was to cherish, provide for, and ensure that he knew that he was loved unconditionally. Three and a half years later, God blessed me with another miracle, a daughter. Like her brother, she was beautiful. Her big blue eyes, chubby cheeks, and no hair still lit up the room and the moment she was placed in my arms, she also stole my heart. They were both picture perfect. My daily prayer was to instill the same beliefs, morals, and blessings that were bestowed upon me by my parents. They were allowed to spread their wings and explore the positive things in life. Today, I can say I planted the seed and they have both made wonderful life decisions for themselves.

They are not only dedicated to their own families, but continue to contribute to society and touch other people's lives. My son, who is an electrical engineer, dedicates his free time to coaching hockey and is a wonderful mentor for any player that is placed under his wing. He is highly respected and loved, not only by the players, but the parents and the community that he lives in. My daughter is an entrepreneur and even though she owns her own dental hygiene clinic and a satellite clinic, she is always giving back to the community. She plays a major role in the community by always providing services for the not-so-fortunate and supports an organization called "Gift from the Heart"! Even though they have grown and matured into beautiful adults and parents themselves, one thing is for sure: they may have outgrown my lap, but they will never outgrow my heart.

They both paid it forward and blessed me with four amazing grandchildren. They both have a son and daughter and they are growing up to be such beautiful souls. They are very loving, caring and affectionate. Each one of them has a beautiful personality and is unique in their own way, but definitely complement each other.

However, looking back in time at all the turmoil in my life, I had continued to maintain a full-time career and educating myself, always learning and staying up-to-date on the latest technology. No matter how busy my life was, I always ensured that my children were the number one priority in my life. Their lives were equally busy with school and activities outside of school. One of my main priorities was to ensure that they would have a wonderful life by taking them to church and exposing them to the same beliefs, morals, and blessings that were bestowed upon me by my parents.

I was blessed to be born into a beautiful loving family and Christian home. My parents blessed me with four siblings: three sisters, and one brother, who are my world. I recall that as a little girl, my mother would gather us together every morning before we would go to school and pray with us. She would always ask for God's guidance and protection over us as we went to school and started our daily routines. My dad, many times unknown to my mom, would be listening to her praying and he would be moved to tears listening to her cries for his children, whom he loved dearly. We were loved unconditionally and when one hurt, we all hurt.

I have so many fond memories of my life growing up as a child and adult. Our parents were very protective, ensured that we were cared for in every area of our lives, and only wanted the best for us. I recall telling my dad that I was getting married and he was to give me away in marriage. He said no. My heart was crushed. It was every girl's dream for their dad to walk them down the aisle. His response was, "If you have a life of hardship, I don't want to be responsible."

But one of my most precious moments that I will always hold near and dear to my heart was the day I decide to be baptized in water. This was a part of my Christian walk and my heart's desire to follow Jesus (Mark 16:16). The church was full to capacity and they had to use the overflow. When it was time for me to walk down the aisle and be baptized, I stepped out of my seat and my dad stepped out at the same time. He took my arm and placed it in his and whispered in my ear, "I kept the best for last. I didn't give you away in marriage and now you know why. I know you are safe with God." Oh, my heart! He walked me to the water fountain and placed my hand in one of the elders of the church and when I stepped out of the fountain, my mom was waiting on the other side for me. There weren't too many dry eyes in the church, something that people never witnessed before. My father was a wonderful example of God's love for his children!

After years of emotional, mental, and physical abuse and dropping to my lowest weight ever, I completely understood what my dad meant by a life of hardship. He was a very wise man and followed his heart's intuition. In 2008, I walked away from my marriage of 34 years, which took me many years to decide. I did not want my children to grow up in a home without a father figure and I had strong religious beliefs about divorce. Upon making my decision, the most painful part was finding the courage to break the news to my parents since I did not want to disappoint them, knowing their religious beliefs. But to my surprise, they supported me and told me it was my time to be happy and they were there for me no matter what. These words made my broken heart swell with happiness. The next step was breaking the news to my children. They were very supportive and said, "Mom, you should have moved on years ago! You could have done it on your own." I was overwhelmed by tears, joy, and happiness. I felt that I had their permission to move on and start a new life. I started my new life. I found myself trying to find Judy again, who I lost somewhere in the process.

I spent four wonderful years alone in my little safe haven again, working, attending church, visiting family and friends, and always meditating on God's Word and being spiritually fed daily. I worked very hard with my doctor to help with my weight gain, restore my physical strength, my self-esteem, independence, and confidence, and I succeeded in doing so. I was so proud of my accomplishments, both physical, mentally, emotionally, and spiritually. This girl that was lost in the midst of the storm was finally on the road to recovery. Every day I woke up with a song in my heart, a smile on my face, and was ready to take on whatever God had prepared for me. Finally, I was able to look in the mirror and take back what I allowed to be stolen from me.

In 2012, I found myself in a relationship thinking, "This is it! This is the way a relationship is supposed to be: love, laughter, date nights, family time, and traveling." But, much to my surprise, I was once again brought to my knees doing the same thing I did in my first relationship. I was emotionally and mentally drained and I suffered massive weight loss. I was always protecting myself with a happy face, but in the interim, dying inside again. I always said I wore two faces: a work face and a home face!

During this time, I lost one of my precious mentors, my dear father, my job, and another relationship. I became very weak emotionally and mentally and the only thing I had was my spirituality. My world was crushed and I felt like there was no hope. I wondered how I would ever recover and live my life that God had so graciously blessed me with. I would soak my pillow at night with tears and would look up to the sky and call out to my dad. I would say, "If you are up there looking down, please send me a sign." I had suppressed and internalized all of the pain from all the years of mental, emotional and physical abuse that led me to shut down completely. As much as I believed and prayed, I made a decision that I take total ownership of. I decided to end my life. I was totally raw from the inside out. On December 29, 2015, I tried to commit suicide. I wrote a note to my children, mom, and siblings and told them I was sorry for what I was doing, but I did not have the strength to continue on. I recall lying on the bed before I lost consciousness with the suicide note beside me and tears streaming down my face, knowing what I was doing was morally wrong and unbiblical.

But God had other plans for my life. He had guardian angels looking out for me. Angels unaware! My siblings, with the help of their spouses who live across Canada, became very worried about me. The last thing I did before I laid on my bed was text my children and siblings the same message. They started calling each other and asking if they had heard from me, realizing that they all received the same message. This was a red flag and out of character for me. They started reaching out for help since my closest sibling lived six hours away and a family member lived about fifteen minutes from me. My one family member came to my home with her friend and they tried everything, but could not get into the house. They were certain that I was in there and would not give up. Finally, a decision was made to contact the police. The police, as well as the first responders, were dispatched to my home. They kicked the door in and found me. My heartbeat was very shallow and the paramedics worked on me and then transported me to a hospital where I stayed for several days.

I recall waking up wondering where I was, strapped in a bed, and unable to put my hands to my face. I was later moved to the hallway with the freedom of being able to move. I laid on a stretcher for a day and a half and watched everyone coming and going. During that time, I recall a beautiful young girl lying on a stretcher in the hallway next to me with her mom sitting beside her. She asked me my name and why I was there. She told me her story and my first words to her were, "Do you believe in God?" She responded that she wasn't truly aware of God and asked if I believed. I walked over to her and gave her a *Promise and Blessings* book filled with Scripture verses for every day of the year. We exchanged hugs and her mother was brought to tears. She said, "You are an angel and I hope this will help her." I said, "Believe me, it will." In the midst of everything that was going on in my world, God gave me the strength to reach out and share my faith.

The next day I was still lying there after several meetings with the doctors, waiting for them to make a decision about whether I was going to be discharged or not. However, I knew in my heart that God had a plan for me and once again

I was waiting for his confirmation. My loved ones had come to visit, and they were all sitting on the stretcher with me when the doctor arrived. He looked at me and said, "You definitely have a lot of family, support, and love. We are going to discharge you and we don't see any reason for you to be here. What you had done was out of character and you were crying out for help, but none of your family or friends recognized it." These were the same words the police had told my relative and friend when they found me and my suicide note. 'She was crying out for help and did not want to die.' I stood up and gave him the biggest hug ever, thanked him, introduced him to my family, and whispered, "God is good." After all these years of pain and turmoil, I became a pro at hiding my feelings and always making everyone think that my world was perfect. When I was leaving the hospital, I stopped and gave the beautiful girl that I met a big hug and wished her well. She hugged me back and said, "Thank you, I keep reading them over and over again. I love it!" I told her to keep reading, I would be praying for her, and she would find her way.

My recovery wasn't an easy one, but with the support of my family, friends, church family, and doctor, but most importantly my faith in God, I made it back to the road of recovery. I spent time with my precious mother and siblings where I felt loved and safe. Many nights I would wake up and my mom would be lying beside me, tears pouring down her face, telling me everything was going to be okay. "You are a strong girl, Judy, and you will rise again and even better than you ever was." A praying mother, siblings, extended family, and friends always told me that I was "Compton

Strong!" (Compton was my maiden name) They never ceased in praying, encouraging, and ensuring that I was on the road to recovery.

As strong as my faith was, this was one time that God had shown me that the family that prays together, stays together. Also, don't give up on the brink of a miracle. Psalm 4:8 and Philippians 4:19 encouraged me to rest in his promise that He would supply all my needs according to His riches in glory. I was also to rejoice, receive, request, reap, and continue to run the race with faith, hope, and patience. (Acts 20:24) I learned not to be discouraged and never give up when facing challenges in my life. God would give me strength to help me cope with adversity and He was preparing me with all the spiritual tools that I needed to raise again.

Yes, I may have lost a job making six figures a year, had to lower my standard of living and take a lower paying job. I learned to adapt to a new lifestyle of not living in a four-bedroom home in Canada and a vacation home in Phoenix, Arizona with two vehicles and all the luxuries that anyone could ask for, to sleeping on an air mattress for six months with lawn chairs for furniture, my clothes in the back of my car, and my furniture in storage, until I knew what my plans were for this new journey that I was about to embark upon. It has taught me that the material things of this world were nothing compared to being happy, content, and knowing what He has prepared for me. It wasn't how big the house was, but how happy the home was; a home combined with faith, family, and friends.

I prayed for months telling God what my heart's desire was, holding onto the spiritual tools that he gave me. My prayer was to find a job, not knowing it would be a career change, to stay in the city that I was currently living in where I was very happy and content, and to find a church where I could be spiritually filled. However, I told **God** I would go where He wanted me to go.

During the trying times of waiting and praying for God's answers and direction, I discovered that sometimes God takes us in a different direction, but it turns out to be the best road ever taken. God taught me that it was okay to be alone, because in the stillness I would find hope, peace, and solitude. God also taught me that it was better to walk alone than to go in the wrong direction. I never wanted to lose sight of the second chance that He has given me and never take one day for granted. In every situation or separation there will be always changes, like having to let go of old friends and create new ones. I surround myself with positive people who would support me in the good and not so good times, always remembering that a real friend sticks closer than a brother. (Proverbs 18:24)

Once again, my prayers were answered and were another confirmation of God's promise to be obedient to his word. Be still and know that I am God! (Psalm 46:10). One of the first steps on the path to my new journey was a career change. After working as a professional supply chain buyer for almost thirty years, I soon found out that change wasn't always negative, as it opened my eyes and heart to a brand-new world. It gave me the opportunity to see the possibilities of giving back to society in a different working environment.

To be able to pay it forward and to share in the success stories of others has become a ministry for me. However, the struggles and trials in my life helped me to truly understand what the real world is capable of doing to us. The new friendships that I have made with my work and church community have been a blessing in my life and very near and dear to my heart.

God taught me that forgiveness was healing. Letting go of the anger and resentment would not only make me stronger mentally, emotionally, and spiritually, but it would give me that inner peace within my heart. I have learned, in the different seasons of my life, that the heart is very fragile. It is one of the most powerful organs; it breaks, it heals, and it becomes stronger again. I found that one of the most courageous decisions that I ever had to make was not only to forgive, but to finally let go of what was hurting my heart and soul. That doesn't mean that the damage never existed, it means the damage no longer controls my life. It's a process and the healing took time, with patience and love. It is a wonderful blessing to know that my heart is set free and there are no chains on me. My prayer was for God to create in me a clean heart and renew a right spirit within me (Psalm 51:10).

Today, I can proudly say that I am grounded once again in my life and the journey is that much sweeter. I not only fill my heart and soul with spiritual food, but I have also learned how to take care of my physical body. I was introduced to a wellness program by a beautiful lady on LinkedIn. All she knew was that my profile read, "Seeking new opportunities." She reached out to me, like so many others who offered their prayers and support. She has been a big part of my wellness journey and with her support and ongoing love we set some goals. One of my biggest goals was to run a 5k. I am so proud to say that I not only ran the race, but I crossed the finish line at the tender age of 61 years old with hundreds of people cheering me on when I crossed that finish line.

I learned many lessons in my life's journey: to stay positive, keep fighting, stay brave, ambitious, and focused, but most of all, stay strong. Reach out to others who are suffering and not internalize, suppress, and stay silent. Speak up, seek help, and stop the addiction of falling into the same relationships. Find someone who you feel safe with and can trust, but always keep God in the palm of your hand. Don't allow the silence to steal your joy, or maybe even your life. Take ownership for your own actions, but always remember that you are not responsible for anyone else's. God gave us something very beautiful and precious. I don't and won't allow my wrong decision to end my life, control my destiny, or let it be a stigma. It has been one of many life's lessons for me that helped me to realize I could have missed it all. What I have today, some people are praying for and their lives may have been taken way too soon.

One thing is for certain, I am humbled and honored to have been given this opportunity to share my life's journey and not afraid of being judged or rejected. Yes, I have been judged and rejected, and even after sharing my story, I may still be. But, for me, it has been cleansing, healing, and I feel free from the chains that were binding me. My prayer is that I can be a living testimony and touch lives and let others know that if it wasn't for the valleys that I had to go through,

I would never appreciate the mountaintop. Not every day will I be on the mountaintop, but I have come to learn that sometimes I need to be in valley to appreciate the mountaintop and never lose sight of what God has done for me. It's like the poem I have read many times while going through my own pain and grief and shared with friends and family whenever the opportunity presents itself: "IT'S IN THE VALLEY I GROW!"

About the Author – Judy Denney

I was born in the beautiful scenic town of Englee, Newfoundland, Canada. Even though I have spent most of my life living away, I have always kept my roots closed to my heart.

I have worked in both public and private sector, from Dental Assistant, Tax Advisor, and Professional Buyer in Oil & Gas, Mining Sector and Administrative Assistant. Each career has been very rewarding and fulfilling. It has provided me with the knowledge and resources to give back to society in many capacities. To be able to pay it forward by helping others succeed in life either in career growth, wellness or finding a greater purpose for their lives. To share in the success stories of others has become a ministry for me. I contribute it to my own life's journey and how I have been able to rise above the different seasons in my life.

I am the proud mother of two amazing children, and four grandchildren who are not only my world, but my most precious treasures.

In my free time, I love to golf, sports fanatic, reading, spending time with family, friends, church and traveling. I have now found a new gift in my free time. "Writing!" It is not only fitting for me to show my gratitude to Mr. Mike Rodriguez for introducing me to this beautiful gift, but encouraging me to always trust in God and He would help me open my heart, find my voice and be able to share my story.

Contact Information:
LinkedIn: linkedin.com/in/judy-a-denney-6a045055
Instagram: stayhumble_staykind

Chapter 6 – My Heart Set Free – No Chains on Me!

Chapter 7

Making a Difference
By Glenn Keller

I've heard that the two most important days of our life are the day that we were born and the day we find out why. The day I was born is easy, especially since I've had 57 birthdays. It actually took some time to find out or to recognize why I was born. I was born to make a difference. In contemplating what I would write, I started thinking about where my desire to make a difference first manifested itself. As I began to search the deep recesses of my mind, I became really curious about when and where this desire came from. It really didn't become apparent to me until 2009. However, it started with the 2008 Presidential Election. Five minutes after the election results were in and President Obama had won, I got a call from my elderly mother wanting to go to the inauguration. Although it was freezing cold in Washington, D.C., the day of the inauguration was an experience none of us will ever forget. We were there to be apart of the first African American to be sworn in as President of the United States of America. This was something my mother could not have imagined happening in her lifetime. The entire campaign had been about change and getting involved. The air was filled with the excitement, enthusiasm, and the very real possibilities for change and for people to make a difference. Something that had been in the back of my mind was now in the forefront of my mind. It was now awake and I knew it was my purpose and the plan God had for my life. When my wife Tomlyn and I returned to Texas, acquired a building, went through our closets, and gathered all the clothes that we could, we were off to Cleburne, Texas with seven or eight huge garbage bags of clothing to start what came to be known as *Making A Difference Ministries Outreach Center*. The first attempts at making a difference was to provide clothing to those in the community that may have been in need.

You see, we didn't even start out being residents of Texas. We were both born and raised in Louisiana. As people around the world know, Hurricane Katrina came roaring through Louisiana with a vengeance in August 2005. That's right, we were evacuees of Hurricane Katrina. We were far from being the only ones that evacuated Louisiana to settle in Cleburne, Texas. The citizens of Cleburne came together in an unbelievable way and showed an incredible amount of love to those of us that were unable to return to our homes. I would say we were fortunate but that wouldn't be entirely true. We were blessed beyond measure. People brought food every day. Clothing was provided to us. We were even given temporary housing. When I say blessed, we were blessed in a way that only God could work. I started working at a hotel the day after I arrived in Texas. It wasn't long when my previous experience with The Department of Health and Human Services in Louisiana allowed me to get a better job in Texas. Within 8 months we had purchased a home in Burleson, Texas. There had been so much love shown towards us and so much given to us during our time of need that we felt like it would only be appropriate for us to give back.

Out of that effort grew *The Making A Difference Ministries Live Prayerline*, which still exists today at 6am CDT seven days a week. There was a time that I was called to pastor a church. The members of the church surely thought I had lost my mind when I told them I was interested in having members. My interest was in building a team of Difference Makers. You see, there is nothing deep and philosophical about the title *Making A Difference*. It means just what it implied and that was to make a difference. I was hoping to build a team of those who could look at a situation, and after seeing that things were not meant to be that way, they would be prepared to take action to change it for the better.

There are two situations that stand out to me and they both occurred when I was proudly serving in the United States Army. I was an 18-year-old Private First Class that had just arrived in Bamberg, Germany, 5.124 miles from my first assignment after completing training. I worked in a communications center where we worked three shifts, the same way you would on any civilian job. The majority of us lived in the barracks. We also ate in the mess hall or chow hall, depending on what you wanted to call it. It may not seem like a big deal, however if you wanted to eat lunch when it was your turn to work nights, you would have to interrupt your sleep in order to eat, (free at the mess hall) or go to the base cafeteria and pay for your food. Since we performed shift work we should have received Basic Allowance for

Quarters (BAQ), which meant we would have received pay so that we could eat at our leisure, wherever we wanted to eat, without interrupting our rest. Well, we weren't getting BAQ and I was told that it had been tried and that the powers-to-be would never approve it. I found the regulations that covered being eligible for BAQ, found we were eligible, and the lowest man on the totem pole stated our case to the First Sergeant. To make a not-too-long story short, it wasn't long after that we were all receiving BAQ. I assume it would be fair to consider that making a difference. At the time I didn't see it as making a difference, I saw it as getting us some money so we could eat when and where we wanted to.

When I came back from Germany I returned to civilian life. After finding it difficult to find adequate employment, I returned to the Army. There is more to this story in my previous book, but this is a different story. This time I was in training as a Chaplin's Assistant in New Jersey. During this time, I was worshipping with The Seventh Day Adventist Church. While in training I met two other Adventists. Until we found a worship service, we observed the Sabbath in the barracks. It wasn't long before we found an Adventist service off base. We informed our Drill Sergeant that we had found a service that we would like to attend and were seeking permission to do so. On Friday, the day before the Sabbath, the Drill Sergeant did something that, until that point, he had never done. He called an inspection for the entire barracks for the next morning, which was not only Saturday, but was the day that we recognized as the Sabbath. The inspection was for everybody in our unit and we were specifically told that we were going to need to participate in that inspection instead of going to church and keeping the Sabbath.

My new friends asked me, "What are we going to do?" Me? Really? The only thing I could think of in keeping with our faith was to prepare our lockers, beds, and areas for inspection that Friday evening. So, we did just that and we slept on the floor to keep from disturbing our respective areas. During the actual inspection, we were downstairs waiting to see if we would be allowed to attend church. After the Drill Sergeant finished the inspection we were called into his office and yelled at really loudly. When he finished denigrating us, he told us to get out of his office and go to church. During the rest of training we were never bothered again about keeping the Sabbath or attending church on Saturday. When my Adventist friends and I had graduated from training and before departing for our assignments, the Drill Sergeant called us back into his office. We couldn't imagine what for. This time, he asked us to sit down. He went on to explain that during every training cycle he would have a Seventh Day Adventist in his unit. And every cycle he would use, what he confessed, was the same tactic on all of them. He always made them do what he wanted them to do despite their desire to keep the Sabbath. As a man of God himself, (not an Adventist) he had been testing everyone's commitment to their faith. He wanted to let us know that we were the first to take a stand for what we believed in. The reason why I share this story as an example of making a difference is this: although none of that experience meant a whole lot at the time, I've learned that oftentimes making a difference will mean taking a stand. In my story, we stood as a group. There are many times when trying to make a difference you will stand alone. It may not be to a Drill Sergeant. It may not even be to a person at all, but the world will test you to see if you're committed to the difference you're trying to make.

My first book was *Moving My Mountains: A Journey to Peace from Codependency*. I was humbled when it became a best-seller. After great counsel from my good friend and publisher, Mike Rodriguez, I didn't talk about being co-dependent. I wasn't claiming that. Instead, I was someone dealing with co-dependent behavior. Writing that book was a cathartic experience for me. Codependency, by definition, is primarily an inability to have a healthy relationship. There was no balance in my relationships and they were often, or I should say, always, one-sided. By the time I finished telling my story, even if I had never sold a book, I came to realize that the next difference I needed to make was in my own life. My self-worth needed a make-over. I actually had to come to realize how important I am. I don't think it was God's will for me to make a difference in the lives of others to my own personal demise. What needed to happen was I needed to become important to me. The desire to make a difference was as strong as ever, but now I realized I could make a difference in the lives of others while maintaining my own life in a healthy and positive way.

Please allow me to share with you the thoughts that went through my head and the conclusions that I came to, based on my faith in God. There is no healthcare professional that substantiated this for me. This time I drew my own conclusions. It started out as a discovery of having codependent behavior. My relationships were one-sided, my life was help, help, help everybody, and I practically ignored the needs of Glenn. I grew up hearing how God didn't make any junk. It may not be in the Scriptures that way, but I whole-heartedly believe it. Although things in my life may have been out of balance, in my heart I knew that I was fearfully and wonderfully made. (Psalm 139:14) There are times that we feel like our minds are playing tricks on us, but we have an enemy whose only desire is to try to overthrow the plan of God for our lives. I know and I know that I know that I was born to make a difference and I bind every spirit that will try to come against the plan of God for my life. I can't even think of a time that the devil was ever able to circumvent the plan of God. I'm going to guess that the enemy knew that if I were to continue ignoring myself and being overly concerned with everything and everybody else, the train would eventually run off of the tracks. Knowing that God's grace is sufficient is one thing, but when you experience the sufficiency of God's grace it is something different. The thorn in my flesh was recognized as co-dependent behavior and I was running all over the place making a difference everywhere and for everyone but me. When it comes to thorns in the flesh, I can hear God telling Paul, "'My grace is sufficient for thee, for my strength is made perfect in weakness.' Most gladly therefore will I rather glory in my infirmities, that the power of Christ may rest upon me." (2 Corinthians 12:9-10)

I was not going to just run around making a difference in people's lives, in communities, and in the world, without having to go through something, without having to experience discomfort and pain. My beliefs are rooted and grounded in God and His Word. I've come to realize there is also a need to believe in the 'me' that God created. I may have flaws, but I learned that oftentimes God uses flawed vessels. I feel like the enemy would leave me to my own devices. The enemy would watch me run myself into the ground. I would be trying to make all these differences everywhere and not replenishing myself and end up losing out or giving up on what I have come to realize was not only my gift, but my 'why'. The desire to make a difference seems to be a noble enough gesture, but it's not a gesture, it's my 'why'. My 'why' I was born. My why God breathed the breath of life into my body. Making a difference is my purpose.

One of my favorite Scriptures is about the man with palsy that was brought to Jesus. There was some murmuring about Jesus telling the paralytic that his sins were forgiven. Jesus responded, "Whether is it easier to say to the sick of the palsy, Thy sins be forgiven thee; or to say, Arise, and take up the bed, and walk." (Mark 2:9) I think about it in different ways. One of the ways is there was a man that was bedridden and couldn't walk. Not only did Jesus tell a man that couldn't walk, to walk, but then Jesus tells him to pick up his bed and walk. Wow! However, this was a man who, a few minutes earlier, couldn't even walk and Jesus is now telling him to carry the thing that had been carrying him. There was no mention of someone offering to take his bed for him. There are times when we are trying to do God's will and there is no help. Times when we take a stand and we are the only one, it seems, taking that stand. I've noticed it when it comes to preachers, myself included. There may be times when God gives us a vision or assignment and we are looking for everyone to jump on board and get excited because we are excited and it doesn't always happen that way. Those are the times you have to trust and believe that what you're doing or about to do is what God has told you to do.

As a young preacher, I woke up one Sunday morning and no sooner had I gotten out of bed than I decided that I didn't want to preach that day. The only thing that made that an issue was that we never knew when our pastor was going to call on us to preach. Allow me to further explain. You see, church service would always start promptly at 11 o'clock. At around 11:30 our pastor would get up from his chair on the pulpit, walk out of the side door of the church, and then enter the church through the front doors. What our pastor was doing was looking for who he would ask to preach that Sunday. I already told y'all I woke up not wanting to preach. I can't even tell you why, I just didn't want to preach. Here was my master plan. I knew our pastor always took that walk at about 11:30, give or take a few minutes, so I wasn't going to show up until about noon, well after the preacher had been selected. Normally I would sit in the pews, however, I was so confident that my plan had worked that at noon I entered the side door of the church and proudly sat on the pulpit.

I was sitting there looking around trying to figure out who might be preaching. I finally realized I didn't really care as long as it wasn't me. Well my pastor was sitting on the other end of the pulpit from where I was sitting and I just happened to look down his way and he was looking back my way. I'm no lip reader, but as he looked in my eyes he mouthed the words I'll never forget. They were, "Will you preach for us today?" Talk about a loaded question. What are you supposed to say to that question? 'No thank you, I believe I'll pass today,' even though that's exactly what I was trying to do. In an almost panic, I grabbed my Bible and went straight down the side wall of the church, passed every pew and into the secretary's office where she was sitting at her desk. There was a little space between her desk and the small closet where we kept the mops, brooms, and cleaning supplies. When I tell you I fell on my knees, I mean I fell on them. I didn't cry out loud, but I did cry out, "Lord I need a Word!" When I got up off of my knees, the secretary, who I believe at the time was about 80 years old, stopped me. Her words to me were, "Baby, if you know God called you to do what He called you to do, it will be all right." I thought for a moment about what she had told me and I walked right back up to the pulpit with an obedient spirit and allowed God to use me.

Don't think there haven't been times I questioned God about this 'making a difference' thing. When at times it seems I'm doing my best to make a difference in a particular situation, to my naked eye nothing seems to be working. Then I remember the words of that church mother who told me at about noon that Sunday morning, "Baby, if you know God called you to do what He called you to do, it's going to be all right."

God told Abram, "Go out from your land, your relatives, and your father's house to the land that I will show you." (Gen 12:1) God told Abram to pretty much leave everything and everybody and to go. What God didn't tell Abram was where he was going. God did tell Abram he would go to a place He would show him. To go takes trusting God. You just leave and somewhere along the way God lets you know where you're going. I sit here searching my mind, unable to even begin to tell you how many times I seemingly stumbled into a situation and was able to somehow, or someway, by the grace of God, make that situation better, or shall I say, make a difference. Did I say seemingly stumbled? The Bible says in Psalms 37:23 "The steps of a good man are ordered by the Lord." There were countless other times in my travels back and forth across this country that I would coincidentally cross the path of some man, woman, boy or girl, who I was able to help make a difference in their life in some way.

My prayer used to be for God to use me. I tend to think now that that approach was flawed. Instead of trying to be used or trying to orchestrate where a difference might need to be made, I came up with a better plan. The new plan was good and it wasn't stressful. All I do now is make myself available to God. I don't have to spend an entire day trying to figure out where God wants me to go and what he wants me to do. By making myself available to God, wherever I am is where he wants me to be. Whatever I'm doing is what God had planned for me to do. I can try to guess or imagine where the greatest need is or where I can do the most good, but making a difference is embedded in my DNA and God knows more about my skill sets than I know about my skill sets. God is forever guiding me to places that He ultimately shows me. (Proverbs 16:9) God wouldn't send a carpenter to do a job where a plumber was needed. When God shows me a place, I'm there because He knows what I was created for. After all, He is The Creator. He is the origin of all the gifts and talents that we possess. I may show up at a place God shows me and my reaction may be, 'God, why me?' God knows more about me and what was placed inside of me. God has hand-picked us for the plans and purposes He has for our lives. God won't send me to do what He gifted someone else to do and vise versa.

There is a gospel song that says "God Specializes." Moses was born to lead the children of Israel out of Egypt. It was for Moses and Moses alone to be chosen to tell Pharaoh to let God's people go. That was done in spite of Moses trying to tell God that he couldn't talk well enough for what he was being asked to do. What about Noah? It wasn't just anyone that could have built a boat on dry land, gather every creature two by two, preach for around 100 years that "It's going to rain," and then spend 40 days and 40 nights in an ark filled with two of every animal. Of all the people on that planet, at that time it had to be Noah. What about David, the little shepherd boy? When Israel needed a king, only God would choose a boy that would replace Saul. David's faith allowed him to kill a giant with a sling and a rock. There is something to be said of God when he uses someone to do something and no one understands and can hardly believe it happened. Only God knew what he had placed inside of David and for what purpose and time He would call on David to use it. In the book of Esther chapter 4 verse 14, we read, "…and who knoweth whether thou art come to the kingdom for such a time as this?" God knew she was in the right place at the right time to fulfill her purpose.

When we determine our "Why" we should embrace it and never doubt it. When we determine the plan and purpose God has for our lives, it may not be utilized when and where we see fit. It's very possible that is because God is planning to use us when and where He sees fit. A few words of a song by *The Brooklyn Tabernacle Choir* goes, "You gave me my hands to reach out to man to show him your love and your perfect plan. You gave me my ears, I can hear your voice so clear, I can hear the cry of sinners but cannot wipe away their tears. You gave me my voice to speak your Word, to sing all your praises to those who never heard. But with my eyes I see a need for more availability. I see hearts that have been broken, so many people to be freed. Lord I'm available to you."

About the Author – Glenn Keller

My name is Glenn C. Keller, Sr and I was born in New Orleans, LA., home of The Mardi Gras and affectionately known as The Big Easy. I have one sister Carol Ann Keller and two sons TaDaro L. Keller and Glenn C. Keller, Jr.

I grew up in church which was not an option back then, and I am grateful. I was educated in the public-school system and graduated from Warren Easton Fundamental High School.

About 10 days following graduation, I enlisted and served in The United States Army. After serving my country, I came home and served my community as a Criminal Sheriff's Deputy. On April 5, 1986, I was ordained and served The Lord as a minister of The Gospel of Jesus Christ. After Hurricane Katrina, I relocated to Burleson, TX, where I founded *Making A Difference Ministries*. The Ministry was about people helping people. Out of that ministry grew our live prayer line which still takes place at 6am every morning 7 days a week.

Fast forward a few years and I was honored to become a Ziglar Certified Speaker and Trainer and I believe that added depth to my ministry by actually giving people a plan of how to set and achieve their goals. I met Mike Rodriguez and with the help of Tribute Publishing was able to become a best-selling author when I wrote, *"Moving My Mountains A Journey to Peace from Codependency."* My future plans include doing everything I can, by the grace and help of God to continue to make a difference in the lives of God's people.

Glenn C. Keller, Sr
P.O. Box 27
Alvarado, TX 76009

Glenn c. Keller, Sr.
504.982.2380 Ph
thegoalsman@gmail.com email
www.thegoalsman.com website

Chapter 7 – Making a Difference

A Better Plan – Stories That Inspire

Final Thoughts

Throughout my life, I have always felt a bigger and better plan for my life, but I have not always been in pursuit of it, mostly because I have been my biggest obstacle. I was often distracted by my current comfort zones through my current routines. They kept me from stepping into my full potential and kept me bound, as a prisoner of mediocrity. I knew that I wanted to pursue my "better plan," I just wasn't focused enough to see it or empowered enough to take action.

After years of very strong feelings that God had something more for me, I only took action to start changing my life, when I chose to have faith and act on God's plan for me. I knew this was the only way to make big changes in my life.

Through His grace, I am a new man. I understand my purpose and I am full of life. I can see Him clearly, and I am stronger than ever.

With regard to purpose, I have always felt that mine was to help others through the gift of speaking. I have always dreamed of becoming a motivational/inspirational speaker, or maybe even a preacher, but for the largest part of my life, I only considered this a dream.
Who was I to do these things?
What credentials or gifts did I have?
These were negative thoughts that I burdened myself with.

So, who am I?
I am a son of our King.

I know Him and He knows me.

Today, all because of Him, and through my obedience to decide, take action and have faith, I am continuing to live my life's dream. I am pursuing my life's goal, and most importantly, my life's purpose to help others build their lives all for the glory of God. Not only do I travel and speak full-time, but I am also pursuing my MDiv at SWBTS to preach around the world.

Believe in God and accept Him and His calling for your life. Have faith and act. You too can realize your better plan as the son or daughter of the same King!

Now Go Forth and Make YOUR Life Exceptional!

- **Mike Rodriguez**

A Better Plan – Stories That Inspire

About Mike Rodriguez

Mike Rodriguez is a professional speaker, a master trainer and a global evangelist. He is CEO of Mike Rodriguez International, LLC, a professional speaking, training and global ministry organization. Besides being a Best-Selling author, he is a highly sought-after motivator and a leadership, change, and sales expert. Mike and his wife Bonnie also own a publishing company and they still manage to spend quality time with their five daughters, all while Mike is studying for his Master's Degree in Divinity. Previously at DTS (in 2017) and st SWBTS (2018) Mike is a former showcase speaker with the original Zig Ziglar Corporation and was selected as their key speaker for the 2015 Ziglar U.S. Tour.

Mike delivers performance-based seminars and trainings and has authored several books which have been promoted by Barnes & Noble. He has been featured on CBS, U.S. News & World Report, Success Magazine, Fast Company and Business Insider. He has lectured at Baylor University, UNT, K-State Research and UGA. His clients include names like Hilton, Bank of America, McDonald's Corporation, the U.S. Army, and the Federal Government. As a people expert, Mike has trained thousands around the world.

Everyone faces challenges; Mike believes that through faith and action, you can overcome the challenges in your life to attain your goals and become who God has called you to be.

Mike has been happily married since 1991 to Bonnie, the love of his life and together they have five beautiful daughters.

A Better Plan – Stories That Inspire

As a world-renowned speaker,
Mike has experience working with people
from all walks of life.

You can schedule Mike Rodriguez
to speak, inspire or train at your next event.
Go to:
www.MikeRodriguezInternational.com

Other products available by Mike Rodriguez:

Finding Your WHY

8 Keys to Exceptional Selling

Break Your Routines to Fix Your Life

Lion Leadership

Think BIG Motivational Quotes

Walking with Faith

A Bigger Purpose

Trusting in Him

and

The Power of Breaking Routines
(Audio Course from Nightingale Conant)

A Better Plan – Stories That Inspire

Disclaimer & Copyright Information

Some of the events, locales, and conversations have been recreated from memories. In order to maintain their anonymity, in some instances, the names of individuals and places have been changed. As such, some identifying characteristics and details may have changed.

Although the authors and publishers have made every effort to ensure that the information in this book was correct at press time, the authors and publishers do not assume and hereby disclaim any liability to any party for any loss, damage, or disruption caused by errors or omissions, whether such errors or omissions result from negligence, accident, or any other cause. Each author is responsible for the content of each story.

All quotes, unless otherwise noted,
are attributed to the respective Authors or to the Holy Bible.

Cover illustration, book design and production
Copyright © 2018 by Tribute Publishing LLC
www.TributePublishing.com

"Go Forth and Make Your Life Exceptional" ™
is a copyrighted trademark of the Author, Mike Rodriguez.

Scripture references are copyrighted by www.BibleGateway.com
which is operated by the Zondervan Corporation, L.L.C

*"I can do ALL THINGS through Christ
who strengthens me."
Philippians 4:13*

NOTES

NOTES

NOTES

CPSIA information can be obtained
at www.ICGtesting.com
Printed in the USA
BVOW08s0823040418
512448BV00001B/68/P